Complete EnglishSmart

Grade 5

Desmond Gilling

ISBN : 978-1-894810-68-5

Printed in China

Complete EnglishSmart Contents

Integrated Practice

1 Cats

When a house cat sits on your lap purring, it is hard to believe that this cuddly, furry animal could belong to the same family as the sabre-toothed tiger. The first cat was likely the *Miacis*, a small weasel-like meat eater that dates back about sixty million years. The Miacis would not have resembled today's cat, as it was likely an ancestor to the dog and possibly the bear as well. The first cat-like ancestor, the *Dinictis*, dates back about 10 million years.

The early cat family was split into two distinct groups: the *sabre-toothed tigers* and *true cats*. The sabre-toothed tigers were big, powerful animals that roamed the earth for nearly 35 million years. They have been extinct for nearly 12,000 years. The second group, true cats, can be further divided into three categories: big cats (lions, tigers, jaguars, leopards), small cats (felines), and cheetahs. The cheetah is in a classification of its own because it developed separately, becoming the fastest animal on earth capable of speeds of up to 100 kph.

The small cat is a broad classification and includes the lynx, the bobcat, the cougar, and other similarly sized members.

Both big cats and small cats use similar methods of hunting. The leopard will stalk its prey and upon catching it, deliver a fatal bite to the back of the neck bringing quick death to its victim. Small cats, even domestic cats, are capable of similar hunting methods. A house cat will lay in waiting for an unsuspecting bird to land and then pounce on it or it may contain a mouse in its claws and deliver the fatal bite.

The 41 breeds of domestic cats are so popular that many have become famous. Among these superstar cats are *Morris*, the star of television commercials, *Felix* of cartoon fame, Dr. Seuss's *Cat in the Hat*, and *Garfield*.

Recalling Details

A. For each statement, fill in the blank with the best fact from the choices given.

1. The first cat dates back _~~10 million~~_ years.
   30 million   60 million   5 million   250,000

2. The first cat was a weasel-like meat eater called a _Dinictis_.
   Feline   Sabre-toothed tiger   Miacis   (Dinictis)

3. The sabre-toothed tigers roamed the earth for _35._ years.
   35 million   80 million   100,000   500,000

4. Sabre-toothed tigers have been extinct for _12,000_ years.
   100,000   50,000   60,000   12,000

5. Cats are divided into two main groups: _big and small_
   fierce and tame   big and small   striped and plain   lions and tigers

6. The _____ type of cat has its own classification.
   leopard   tiger   (cheetah)   lion

7. The lynx, bobcat, and cougar are members of the _____ group.
   big cat   forest cat   small cat   fierce cat

8. Both big cats and small cats are similar _____.
   runners   hunters   pets   breeds

9. There are _____ different kinds of domestic cats.
   85   104   (41)   14

10. The fastest cat, clocked at up to 100 kph, is the _____.
    lion   (cheetah)   lynx   panther

Common and Proper Nouns

- Common nouns name non-specific persons, places, or things.

  Examples: house, girl, boy, dog, store, bicycle

- Proper nouns name specific persons, places, or things.

  Examples: Atlantic Ocean, Christopher Columbus, Ontario Place

B. Underline the proper nouns and circle the common nouns in each sentence below.

There are 14 common nouns and 14 proper nouns.

1. The students travelled to Ottawa by car.

2. Mr. Smith taught at Maple Road Public School for twenty years.

3. The tourists from Japan visited Niagara Falls and took the Maid of the Mist boat ride.

4. The boys played soccer while the girls played baseball.

5. Jenny and her friend Susan were in the school play, A Christmas Story.

6. Don't step in the puddle by the bottom step.

7. The CN Tower is one of the tallest structures in North America.

8. Mr. Jones travelled to England and visited Buckingham Palace.

Building Vocabulary – Words in Context

- We can understand the meanings of unfamiliar words by examining the context in which the words are used.

- Context refers to the meaning of the sentence in which a word is used. From the meaning of a sentence, we can understand the meanings of the unfamiliar words used in that sentence.

C. In the spaces provided, write the underlined words in the passage that match the meanings.

MEANING	UNDERLINED WORD
1. well-known	_____
2. unaware	_____
3. type	_____
4. no longer exists	_____
5. specific, special	_____
6. wide range	_____
7. strong	_____
8. was formed	_____
9. tame	_____
10. ways of doing	_____
11. hunt	_____
12. well-liked	_____

The "Horseless Carriage" (1)

Just <u>imagine</u> a world without the automobile. To visit a friend, you might take a leisurely walk for two or three hours. Long trips would be by train or horse and carriage. You would likely live in the city or town and be within walking distance of the things you need. Today, many people live in <u>suburbs</u> or in rural areas that, a hundred years ago, would have been considered too far from the everyday amenities. The <u>invention</u> of the automobile changed not only where people lived but also how they lived, and what they did with their leisure time.

The quest to replace the horse and carriage goes back to the early 1770's. Frenchman Joseph Cugnot built a steam-powered three-wheeler, but <u>critics</u> claimed that it was too slow and that it was no match for the horse. It wasn't until the 1850's that internal combustion engines <u>powered</u> by gas and air appeared on the scene. This was an <u>improvement</u> over the steam engine, but it was Nicholas Otto who <u>perfected</u> an internal combustion engine that was light and efficient enough to be used in a transport vehicle. It <u>paved</u> the way for the swift <u>development</u> of the early automobile.

In 1865, Karl Benz, a German engineer, built the first <u>successful</u> gasoline-powered automobile. Like Cugnot's design, it was a three-wheeler, and with the Otto engine, it was <u>capable</u> of speeds of up to nine miles an hour. In 1890, Benz built a four-wheeled vehicle which he displayed in America. It was this automobile that <u>inspired</u> the Duryea brothers, originally <u>bicycle</u> <u>mechanics</u>, to build the first American-made automobile in 1893.

The first automobile to be sold in America was purchased in 1896 and the only thing that remained to be figured out was how to mass-produce them so that everyone could afford one. Once that was accomplished, there would be great changes in the American way of life.

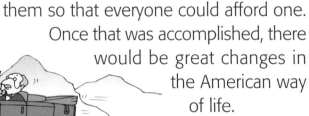

Fact or Opinion

- *Facts are based on exact information from the passage. Opinion is your personal view based on the facts from the passage.*

A. Place "F" for fact or "O" for opinion beside each statement.

1. _____ It might take 2 hours to reach a friend's house.

2. _____ The effort to replace the horse and carriage began in the 1770's.

3. _____ Cugnot built a steam-powered three-wheeled vehicle.

4. _____ Many people today live in suburbs.

5. _____ Without the automobile, travel would not be as easy as it is today.

6. _____ The first gasoline-powered car was built by Karl Benz.

7. _____ Benz was lucky that he had the Cugnot engine to work with.

8. _____ Benz displayed his four-wheeled car in America.

9. _____ The Americans were impressed with the Benz car.

10. _____ The Duryea brothers were influenced by the Benz car.

11. _____ In 1896 the first automobile was sold in America.

12. _____ Mass production was necessary to make cars cheap enough for everyone.

Your Opinion

B. Answer the questions.

1. Why do you think many people were hesitant to replace the horse and carriage with the automobile?

   _____

   _____

2. What was the most important advancement in developing the car?

   _____

   _____

Verbs

- *Verbs are often action words. They tell what something or someone has done.*
  Example: *The boy jumped over the fence.*
  In this case the verb is "jumped" since it tells what the boy did.

- *Verbs are sometimes non-action words. They state that something exists.*
  Example: *The food is on the table.*
  In this case the verb is "is". Notice that there is no real action here.

C.   Write "A" if the verb is an action verb or "N" if it is a non-action verb.

1.   The steam-powered three-wheeler was no match for the horse.   _____

2.   Karl Benz built the first gasoline-powered automobile.   _____

3.   The car sped down the street.   _____

4.   It then made a sharp turn and disappeared in no time.   _____

5.   The hockey player shot the puck into the net.   _____

6.   John is the tallest boy in the class.   _____

7.   The girls are in the school play.   _____

8.   Kitty will play Snow White.   _____

9.   The zookeeper feeds the animals at the same time every day.   _____

10.   He usually takes a rest in the late afternoon.   _____

D.   Place your own choice of verb in each space to complete the sentences below.

The students 1._____ in the schoolyard until the bell rang. On hearing the bell, the teacher 2._____ them to come inside. There 3._____ still a lot of noise in the hallway. Finally, they 4._____ quiet. The teacher 5._____ the students to take out their notebooks and 6._____ the words on the board.

Building New Words

- *Most words have other forms depending on how they are used in a sentence. For example, if you want to make a noun out of the verb 'divide', you would change it to 'division'.*

   Here are some examples of new words that can be built from existing words:

move − movement	associate − association
final − finalize	begin − beginning

E. **For each case, find the underlined word in the passage that shares the same root with the word in the list below. Write it in the matching space.**

	GIVEN WORD	UNDERLINED WORD
1.	inspiration	
2.	capability	
3.	pavement	
4.	critical	
5.	inventor	
6.	imagination	
7.	develop	
8.	perfection	
9.	cycling	
10.	improve	
11.	success	
12.	powerful	
13.	suburban	
14.	mechanical	

The "Horseless Carriage" (2)

Although the first automobile was built in Germany, it was the Americans that figured out a way to <u>mass</u>-produce it. The goal was to build automobiles in such a way that it was cost-effective so that the money saved in <u>manufacturing</u> could be passed on to the consumers. As a result, there would be a reasonably priced car that everyone could <u>own</u>.

In 1893, Henry Ford built his first car based on the Benz model. Benz continued to build expensive cars in Europe for upper class purchasers. Ford had a better <u>idea</u>. He wanted to build cars for everyone. Ford visited a slaughterhouse and watched as the butchers cut the cattle up in an assembly line with each station chopping off a particular portion of beef. Ford decided to apply this method to the production of cars and the automobile assembly line was born – a method still used today.

In 1908, Ford produced the Model "T" which was a simple family car without the fancy <u>trappings</u> found on German cars. In 1913, he created his assembly line and the cars began to roll out. The more he produced, the lower the prices were until he managed to get the price of his Model "T" down to about $285.00. In 1914, Ford paid his workers an incredible $5.00 per day for wages. That was nearly twice the average wage for similar work at that time. Businessmen declared that this was a ridiculously <u>high</u> <u>wage</u> and that he would go broke. Ford reasoned that if he paid his <u>workers</u> enough money, they could afford to buy his cars. By 1924 Ford had sold 2 million cars.

Ford created mass production but it was General Motors that understood marketing. They introduced the yearly model change which enticed buyers to purchase the latest style of car. They also introduced the "payment plan" whereby a buyer could purchase a car on credit and make monthly payments. North Americans fell in love with the automobile and the freedom it created, and soon nearly every <u>household</u> in America owned a car.

Cause and Effect

- *An Effect is the result of something happening or of something being done. The Cause is what is being done.*

  For example, in "Horseless Carriage" (1), we could say that the invention of the automobile was a "cause" and the "effect" was that it changed the way people travelled.

A. For each case below, you are given either a cause or an effect. Where you have a cause, give an effect and for an effect given, suggest a cause.

1. Effect: Cars would be cheap enough for everyone to own.

   Cause: _____

   _____

2. Cause: Henry Ford visited a slaughterhouse.

   Effect: _____

   _____

3. Effect: The Model "T" dropped in price to $285.00.

   Cause: _____

   _____

4. Effect: Ford's workers could afford to buy his cars.

   Cause: _____

   _____

5. Cause: General Motors introduced the yearly model change.

   Effect: _____

   _____

6. Effect: Purchasers of the automobile could make monthly payments.

   Cause: _____

   _____

   _____

Transitive Verbs, Intransitive Verbs, and Direct Objects

- A Transitive Verb requires more information to make the sentence complete.

  Example: The students need pencils. "Need" is a transitive verb because it requires more information. In this case, the additional information comes in the form of an object which is the receiver of the action of the verb "need".

- An Intransitive Verb is complete and does not need an object to receive the action of the verb.

  Example: The children played. "Played" is an intransitive verb because it is complete in its meaning. It does not require any further information.

- An Object is a noun that is the receiver of the action of the verb.

  Examples: 1. The boy kicked the ball. "Ball" is the object and receiver of the verb action "kicked".
  2. He saw the car coming. "Car" is the object and receiver of the verb action "saw".

B. Write "I" for intransitive and "T" for transitive verbs. Underline the verbs and circle the objects of the transitive verbs.

1. _____ Spectators lined the parade route.

2. _____ We watched the parade from the balcony.

3. _____ The marching band wore bright costumes.

4. _____ The horns played loudly.

5. _____ Clowns handed out candy to the children.

6. _____ Everyone smiled at the dog in costume.

7. _____ The parade lasted for two hours.

8. _____ Most people stayed until the end.

9. _____ Jugglers tossed fiery torches into the air.

10. _____ Clouds filled the sky threatening rain.

11. _____ The leader of the band smiled to everyone.

12. _____ Just as the rain started, the parade ended.

There are 7 intransitive verbs.

Synonyms

- *Synonyms are words that have similar meanings.*

  Examples: large - big   tiny - small

  sad - upset   incredible - unbelievable

C. Complete the crossword puzzle with the underlined words from the passage that are synonyms for the clue words.

Down

1. home
2. making
3. thought
4. lofty
5. employees

Across

A. many
B. have
C. extras
D. earnings

Influenza – More Than Just a Cold

Typically during the winter months, many people come down with what is commonly called the "flu". The symptoms may be mild, like those associated with the common cold or more severe. More often, the symptoms will include fever, chills, headache, and body aches. A person may feel aches in many of his or her joints and experience a loss of appetite.

Usually an influenza attack lasts from four days to two weeks, and although uncomfortable, it does not cause great harm. However, some influenza viruses can be more serious. The influenza virus, depending on what strain, can weaken the body to the point where pneumonia and other diseases can set in. In some cases, particularly for the elderly or people who are already very ill, the flu can be fatal.

From 1918 to 1919, a worldwide influenza epidemic killed 25 million people around the world. This particular strain was one of the five deadliest epidemics of all time. But in 1918 there was no scientific treatment for the infection. Today, antibiotics can protect people from developing pneumonia and other diseases that can follow the flu. Doctors have developed vaccines that can protect people against flu viruses. The problem is that the strains of flu are constantly changing and it is difficult for doctors to keep up with the new influenzas that spread around the world.

The concern over influenza is so great that The Centre for Disease Control and Prevention (CDC) has created a special department to stay on alert to report any new strains of flu the moment they arise. Today, doctors are encouraging people to take flu shots. Although flu shots may not prevent the flu, they could significantly lessen the impact of the virus. Healthcare workers, the elderly, and people with chronic illnesses are encouraged to get their flu shots first.

Recalling Details

A. In the statements below, fill in the blanks with the appropriate words or numbers from the list provided at the end of this section.

The word 1._____ is often used as a short form of the word influenza. Symptoms of influenza may include aches, chills, and 2._____. A person with influenza may experience a loss of 3._____. Severe influenza viruses may lead to 4._____ or other diseases. A worldwide influenza epidemic in 1919 caused 5._____ million deaths, making this epidemic in the top 6._____ of all time deadly epidemics. 7._____ are used today to fight against the development of more serious diseases. To protect people against viruses, scientists have developed 8._____ but these have to change with each new strain. The 9._____ created a special department to deal with all the new viral strains. There are influenza 10._____ available to the general public to help offset influenza. Healthcare workers, the 11._____, and people with chronic 12._____ should protect themselves against influenza.

fever	vaccines	illnesses	antibiotics	5	CDC
25	appetite	flu	pneumonia	shots	elderly

B. Give answers to the following questions.

1. What is the biggest problem the medical community faces today regarding influenza?

   _____

   _____

2. Who are most at risk of serious illness brought on by influenza and why is this so?

   _____

   _____

The Pronoun as the Subject of a Sentence

- A Pronoun is a word that takes the place of a noun. The Subject of the sentence is the doer of the action of the verb. A pronoun can act as a subject of a sentence by taking the place of the subject noun.

  Examples: Susan likes eating cake.   She likes eating cake.

  The boys played football.   They played football.

  Note: If the noun being replaced by the pronoun is plural, the pronoun must be plural.

C. Replace the subject nouns with pronouns.

1. The students were late for class. _____ were late for class.

2. John ate his lunch alone. _____ ate his lunch alone.

3. My friend and I watched television. _____ watched television.

4. Susan wore her new coat. _____ wore her new coat.

The Pronoun as an Indirect Object of a Sentence

- A pronoun can replace a noun as both a Direct and Indirect Object. An Indirect Object answers the question of to whom; a pronoun as a Direct Object is the receiver of the action of the verb.

  Example 1:   Rachel was a new student in the school. The students welcomed her.

  In this sentence the pronoun "her" replaces the noun, Rachel. Since the pronoun directly receives the action of the verb "welcomed", it is a pronoun as direct object.

  Example 2:   Rachel was a new student in the school. The students gave her a warm greeting.

  In this sentence the pronoun indirectly receives the action of the verb and answers the question, "To whom was the action directed?" It is an indirect object.

D. For each statement, underline the pronoun and place the word "Direct" or "Indirect" in the space.

1. Paul gave me the books to read.

2. The students threw him up in the air in celebration.

3. Give her the money.

4. I told him my name.

5. His friends took him out for dinner on his birthday.

Words Often Confused

- *Some words have similar spelling patterns and sounds even though their meanings might be quite different.*

E. Select the appropriate word for each sentence based on the definitions given below. Underline your choice.

● accept	to receive	● addition	something added
except	to be left out	edition	published copies
● altar	a place of worship	● adapt	to adjust to something
alter	to change	adept	to be good at doing something
● berth	a place to sleep	● council	a group
birth	being born	counsel	legal advice
● lay	to put down	● miner	one who works in a mine
lie	to sit back	minor	under a legal age
● role	a part a character plays	● stationary	not moving
roll	to turn about	stationery	things for writing

1. The boy went up to (accept, except) his award.

2. The girl was (adept, adapt) at reading and writing.

3. He read the first (addition, edition) of the school year book.

4. For the long trip, they ordered a (birth, berth) on the train.

5. The (counsel, council) members met once a month.

6. (Lie, Lay) the tablecloth in preparation for dinner.

7. The (miner, minor) was not allowed to buy cigarettes.

8. In the school play, he played the (role, roll) of the villain.

9. The (stationary, stationery) remained (stationary, stationery) on the desk.

10. The high priest placed the sacrifice on the (alter, altar).

Treasures of the Orient (1)

In the 13th century, trade between Europe and Asia was channelled through the "Silk Route", the trade route from China to Constantinople (now Istanbul). The Muslims controlled and restricted trade with the East and the merchants of the Mediterranean were completely cut off from the established trade route. The European merchants wanted the silk, spices, and gold found in the East. So important was this market that the Europeans were willing to go to great expense and trouble to find new trade routes.

The Polo family, merchants from Venice, had made the trip to China which was part of a fourteen-year excursion. Their objective was to bring back marketable goods to be sold in Venice. At the request of the Chinese ruler, the great Kublai Kahn, they were to return to China and bring with them many learned men. Kublai Kahn was interested in learning about the European culture.

The Polo family set out for China in 1271 for what was to be a four-year journey. They crossed Asia Minor (Turkey) and Persia (present-day Iran and Iraq). They stayed for nearly a year in northern Afghanistan likely because of illness. Their journey took them across the Himalayan mountains and the Gobi desert and finally to Shangdu (present-day Beijing) where they were reunited with Kublai Kahn.

The Polos stayed in China for another 17 years and became very wealthy. Marco recorded the events of his travels in a book that told of the riches of the Orient. It was his book that inspired Europeans to share in the wealth by finding a trade route by water that would be quick and profitable. The race to discover a trade route was officially launched.

Recalling Information

A. **Indicate whether each statement is true or false by inserting "T" for true and "F" for false in the space provided.**

1. Europe and Asia once traded through the Silk Route.

2. The Polo family were traders from Rome, Italy.

3. European merchants wanted to sell silk and spices.

4. The Polos made a trip to Asia that lasted 14 years.

5. Kublai Kahn was a famous European leader.

6. Persia was today's Iran and Iraq.

7. The Polos were not interested in trading goods.

8. The Polos were poor merchants.

9. The Polos travelled across the Himalayan mountains.

10. Marco Polo recorded the events of his travels in a book.

11. Polo's book was not interesting to Europeans.

12. Kublai Kahn was not interested in European culture.

13. Istanbul was formerly known as Constantinople.

Making Assumptions

B. **Answer the questions.**

1. Why were Europeans interested in establishing a new trade route by water?

_____

_____

2. What do you think the Europeans could offer for trade in the Orient?

_____

_____

More Work with Pronouns

- Pronouns can replace nouns and express ownership.
  His, her, their, our, your and mine are examples.

C. Place the suitable pronoun in the blank in each sentence.

1. Bill and Jean found _____ home in the suburbs.

2. The boy lost _____ keys when he opened _____ school bag.

3. We are proud of what _____ children have accomplished.

4. You must check _____ name on the voter's list.

5. Susan was happy with _____ report card.

6. The barefoot boy said, "Those shoes are _____ ."

Relative Pronouns - Who, Whom, Which, That

- Relative Pronouns refer to nouns or pronouns that precede them which are called Antecedents.

  Example 1: John, who is ten, is in grade five.
  The pronoun "who" refers to the antecedent noun, "John".

  Example 2: The store, which is located in the plaza, was closed.
  The pronoun "which" refers to the antecedent noun, "store".

  Example 3: He caught the ball that was tossed to him.
  The pronoun "that" refers to the antecedent noun, "ball".

- Note: "who" and "whom" refer to people; "which" refers to things and animals; "that" refers to any antecedent.

D. For each case, choose the appropriate relative pronoun.

1. Paul, which, who _____ is the eldest child in the family, must take care of his little sister.

2. The game, whom, which _____ is played using a game board, was enjoyed by the children.

3. We played with the dog that, who _____ belonged to our neighbour.

4. The boy to whom, which _____ the prize was given was very happy.

Discovering and Using New Words

E. **The words in column A appear in the reading passage. Draw lines connecting the words in column A with the meanings in column B.**

COLUMN A	COLUMN B
channelled ●	● cost
established ●	● to ask for
expense ●	● sent in a direction
excursion ●	● heritage or nationality
objective ●	● joined again
marketable ●	● encouraged
request ●	● made, developed
culture ●	● trip
reunited ●	● purpose
inspired ●	● easy to sell

Using New Words in a Sentence

F. **For each case, compose a sentence of your own using the two new words. Try to show the meanings of the words.**

1. excursion, objective

   _____

   _____

2. channelled, expense

   _____

   _____

3. established, culture

   _____

   _____

4. inspired, request

   _____

   _____

Treasures of the Orient (2)

Europe of the mid-fifteenth century was hungry to establish trade routes by sea to the Far East. They were anxious to bring in exotic goods such as gold, silk, and spices that could be sold at home for great profits.

Portuguese explorers were preparing to sail around Africa in search of a trade route. Christopher Columbus had another idea. He believed that the earth was round and therefore by sailing west, he would eventually reach the Orient. Sponsored by Queen Isabella and King Ferdinand of Spain, he set sail in 1492 with three ships and a crew of 90 men. It is likely that Columbus first landed in one of the Bahama Islands. Columbus named the area the Indies, which came to be known as the West Indies. Columbus did not discover the route to the Orient. Instead, he discovered the Americas (now America).

In 1497 Giovani Caboto, also known as John Cabot, attempted to duplicate Columbus's achievement. His course took him much further north. He landed in Newfoundland and discovered the Grand Banks, one of the world's richest fishing areas, but the route to the East remained undiscovered. Finally, after many more adventurous sailors made attempts to discover the passage, Ferdinand Magellan, a Portuguese navigator, completed his voyage around South America. In late October, 1520, he sailed into the peaceful waters of the Pacific Ocean. By mid-March, Magellan reached the Philippines and the route to the East was officially complete. In a dispute with a group of Filipinos, Magellan was killed. He never realized how important his discovery would be for the world.

Thanks to the interest sparked by Marco Polo's book and the navigational skill of Magellan, two routes to the riches of the Orient were discovered – one in the east and the other in the west.

Drawing Conclusions

A.   Give an answer for each question using the information from the passage.

1. Why did Europeans think that trade with the Orient would be profitable?

    _____

    _____

2. Why were sailors attempting two different routes?

    _____

    _____

3. Why was Columbus's discovery of the Americas important?

    _____

    _____

4. Was John Cabot a successful explorer? Why?

    _____

    _____

5. What was the success of Magellan's voyage?

    _____

    _____

6. What was more important, the discovery of the Americas or finding the route to the Orient?

    _____

    _____

7. State who was the more successful explorer, Columbus or Magellan, and why.

    _____

    _____

The Object in a Sentence

- A Direct Object is the receiver of the action of the verb.

  Example: The boy rode the bicycle.

  "Boy" is the subject (doer of the action) and "bicycle" is the direct object of the verb because it directly receives the action of the verb.

- An Indirect Object answers the question to whom the action of the verb is directed.

  Example: The father gave his son a birthday gift.

  The "son" is the indirect object because he is the person to whom the giving was done. The "gift" would be the direct object because it was the thing that was given.

B. For each underlined object in the following sentences, state whether it is Direct or Indirect. Place "D" or "I" in the space provided.

1. _____ The team members wore their <u>sweaters</u> for the game.

2. _____ People who live in the forest cut <u>trees</u> for shelter.

3. _____ The mother told her <u>daughter</u> stories about her youth.

4. _____ He gave <u>her</u> a ride to school.

5. _____ He asked the <u>person</u> in front of him to move over.

6. _____ They gave the charity <u>money</u>.

7. _____ The father read his <u>son</u> a bedtime story.

8. _____ The library showed the <u>children</u> films on Saturday.

C. Use these nouns to place in the blanks below.

trip	it	way	he	bicycle	drink	Michael	top	bottom	hill	he

1._____ rode his 2._____ up the 3._____.

When 4._____ reached the 5._____, he was very tired. He

took a 6._____ from his water bottle and put 7._____ back

in his knapsack. The 8._____ back down was much easier as

9._____ coasted all the 10._____ to the 11._____.

Word Search Challenge

D. Unscramble the words from the reading passage and place the corresponding letters in the spaces provided.

> To help you there is a definition clue for the scrambled word in parentheses.

| | o | | | e | |

utoser (ways of going)

| | i | | p | | t | |

spetudi (argument)

| | r | | f | | |

tiforp (gains)

| e | | o | | | |

coexit (strange, different)

| | o | | | g | |

evagoy (sailing trip)

E. Imagine that you are a cabin boy working on Magellan's ship. Write a letter home telling of your adventure.

> Use some of the new words you have learned from the passage.

October 1, 1520

Dear _____ ,

_____

_____

_____

_____

_____

_____

_____

Yours truly,

Gypsies – an Endangered Culture

When we use the term "endangered", we are usually referring to endangered species of animals. There is great concern over the many types of animals that are at risk of extinction. There are, however, many cultural groups that face extinction, one of which is the Gypsies of Europe.

The Gypsies originated in India and came to Europe over 600 years ago. They were nomadic people, that is, they were constantly on the move from one country to another. They preferred not to take on steady work but chose temporary work on farms, in construction, or in sales. They lived in caravans rather than homes because caravans are mobile. Originally they were horse-traders, but today most of this trading is done within their group and is not a money-making occupation. Gypsy women traditionally made objects to sell such as clothespins while others were fortune-tellers.

The Eastern European Gypsies were more settled than those in Western Europe. These Gypsies often lived a more stable life in villages. They were entertainers and tradesmen who wore distinctive colourful clothing. Eating together is considered a sign of friendship by Gypsies. They are very conscious of cleanliness, separating their water and cooking utensils from those used for washing and personal hygiene.

The Gypsies are becoming extinct because of assimilation. Many of the younger members of this culture are moving into the mainstream culture. Traditionally, Gypsies have been mistrusted by many people who think of them as dishonest in business. In the past, the work they did was useful and appreciated by society in general. Today, Gypsies are not welcome in many countries. In Germany, they face hostility and in some Eastern European countries such as Romania, Gypsies have been killed. As a result, many young Gypsies have chosen to join the cultures of the countries they inhabit.

The Main Idea

- The Main Idea of a paragraph could provide a summary as to what the writer is discussing in a paragraph.

A. Briefly, in one sentence, write the main idea of each paragraph in the space provided.

Paragraph One

_____

_____

Paragraph Two

_____

_____

Paragraph Three

_____

_____

Paragraph Four

_____

_____

 Drawing Conclusions

B. Briefly state your answer to each of the following questions based on your understanding of the reading passage.

1. Why do some people not like the Gypsies?

_____

_____

2. Why are the Gypsies becoming an extinct culture?

_____

_____

3. Why were the Gypsies thought to be colourful people?

_____

_____

Descriptive Language – Adjectives and Adverbs

- Descriptive words help the reader visualize the objects or actions in a sentence.

  Adjectives describe nouns. They might tell you how big, how many, what kind, or what colour a noun is.

  Adverbs describe verbs. They often explain a detail about the verb in a sentence, such as how an action was done. Adverbs can also describe adjectives or other adverbs.

  Example: *Here is a sentence with no descriptive words – The girl ran.*

- *Here is the same sentence with an adjective and adverb added – The young girl ran swiftly.*

  The word "swiftly" is an adverb describing the way the girl ran.

C. In the following sentences, underline the adjectives and put parentheses ( ) around the adverbs.

1. The long train slowly crossed the highway delaying all the cars.

2. The happy child enthusiastically opened her Christmas gifts.

3. The school children sat quietly at their desks.

4. A loud voice rang out from the crowd.

5. The rock band played loudly for their devoted fans.

D. Rewrite the following sentences adding adjectives and adverbs to make the sentences more interesting.

1. The boys swam in the lake.

   _____

2. The car moved down the road.

   _____

3. The lights of the building were shining.

   _____

4. The man sat in the park.

   _____

Descriptive Language

- *Your writing will be improved by the use of descriptive language. Vivid, colourful language helps the reader visualize people, places and things that you are describing.*

E. Replace the underlined words with more descriptive words from the selection below.

expensive	spacious	thrilled	delicious	visited	stormy	scampered

1. They played football on a <u>big</u> field. _____
2. She received a <u>nice</u> gift. _____
3. The weather was <u>bad</u>. _____
4. They were <u>glad</u> to be invited to the party. _____
5. He <u>ran</u> the length of the basketball court. _____
6. It was a <u>good</u> birthday cake. _____
7. They <u>came to</u> the resort for the first time. _____

F. Fill in the blanks with descriptive words from the selection below. Use a dictionary for unfamiliar words.

steaming	poured	terrified	gleamed	abandoned	drenched	stormy
howled	tightly	skipped	patiently	flashed	booming	subside	arrived

It was a 1._____ night and the wind 2._____ through the trees. The girl held on 3._____ to her little brother's hand as he was 4._____ of the lightning that 5._____ across the sky. Suddenly, after a 6._____ clap of thunder, rain 7._____ down on them. They ran for cover in an 8._____ shack by the roadside. There they waited 9._____ for the storm to 10._____. Before long, the storm ended and the sun 11._____ from the clear sky. Happily the brother and sister 12._____ down the road on their way home. When they 13._____ home, they removed their 14._____ clothing and drank 15._____ hot chocolate.

The Amazing Helen Keller (1)

Helen Keller, born in 1800 in Alabama, USA, would have likely been a very ordinary child if it were not for a sudden illness. At the age of just 18 months, she lost both her sight and her hearing. Later, this illness claimed her ability to speak as well. She had virtually no means of communicating with the outside world.

Distressed and frustrated, Helen grew up to become an unruly child who threw terrible tantrums out of frustration. She became completely uncontrollable – like a wild animal.

The Kellers tried to get help from different doctors but no one could suggest a method of treatment. The Kellers then met Anne Sullivan who agreed to move into the Keller home and teach Helen. The first thing Anne did was discipline Helen. She refused to allow her to eat without using a spoon and, despite her wild tantrums, refused to give in to Helen. She then moved into a cottage with Helen and continued her training without any outside interference.

Anne created codes of communication by tapping on the back of Helen's hand to represent words. Helen tapped back but didn't really understand what she was doing. One morning, when Anne and Helen were pumping water from the well, Anne spelled out the word "water" in the tapping code. At the same time, to reinforce the connection between the tapping and the actual water, Anne poured cold water over Helen's hand. Suddenly, a strange look came over Helen's face. Miraculously, she began to understand. She had finally made the connection that Anne had been striving to achieve. Helen became starved for information. Frantically, she touched everything around her learning new words. The connection to the outside world had finally been re-established. Anne had brought Helen out of the darkness.

Referring to the Facts

A. Place a check mark in the circle that matches the best supporting fact for each statement.

1. Anne came up with a way to communicate with Helen.

   Ⓐ She spoke loudly in her ear.

   Ⓑ She tapped the back of her hand.

   Ⓒ She helped Helen draw pictures of objects.

2. Helen was frustrated with her disability.

   Ⓐ Helen became very quiet.

   Ⓑ Helen tried very hard to co-operate.

   Ⓒ Helen threw tantrums like a wild animal.

3. The breakthrough in learning for Helen came one day.

   Ⓐ They were pumping water.

   Ⓑ Suddenly she could hear again.

   Ⓒ Helen nearly drowned.

4. Helen's disability was a coincidence.

   Ⓐ Helen had a childhood illness.

   Ⓑ Helen had a serious accident.

   Ⓒ Helen was born with her disability.

5. Anne was a strict teacher and disciplinarian.

   Ⓐ Anne was cruel to Helen.

   Ⓑ Anne refused to give in to Helen's tantrums.

   Ⓒ Anne used severe punishment to train Helen.

6. There was no medical solution for Helen's problems.

   Ⓐ Helen took medication for her disability.

   Ⓑ Her family doctor suggested many methods of cure.

   Ⓒ Doctors did not have an answer for Helen's parents.

A Sentence and Its Parts

- A Sentence is made up of two parts: subject and predicate.
  The subject of a sentence is the person, object, or idea being talked about in the sentence. It usually performs the action of the verb.

  Example: The boy fell down.
  "Boy" is the subject of the sentence.

- The predicate is the action (verb) in the sentence.

  Example: The boy fell down.
  "Fell down" is the predicate. The bare predicate (verb) is "fell", the action in the sentence.

B. **In each sentence below, separate the subject and predicate with a vertical line and underline the bare predicate (verb).**

1. The boys and girls played in the yard.

2. Cats and dogs are not always friends.

3. Morning is my favourite time of day.

4. The wind howled through the night.

5. Summer holidays will be here soon.

C. **Circle the bare subject and underline the bare predicate in each of the following sentences.**

The subject of one of these sentences involves more than one word.

1. Getting to school on time was impossible for him.

2. The team arrived late for their game.

3. The waves crashed to the shore as the wind blew.

4. Happiness is eating ice cream.

5. Track and field athletes are a special breed.

Using Similes in Description

- A Simile is a comparison of two things that have some characteristics in common. The words "like" or "as" are used to join the two things that are being compared.

  Examples: He jumped like a rabbit.
  She was as snug as a bug.

D. Complete each sentence by creating a simile comparison.

1. She moved like a _____ in the water.

2. He leaped like a _____ over the fence.

3. The building towered like a _____.

4. The plane soared like a _____.

5. The moon was like a _____ in the sky.

6. He struggled like a captive _____ to get free.

7. The sun shone as a _____ on fire.

8. She slept like a _____.

9. Be quiet as a _____ when you come in the house.

10. The cake was as flat as a _____.

Personification

- Personification is a descriptive technique in which non-human things are given human characteristics.

  Examples: The sun kissed the flowers.
  The wind whispered to the trees.

E. Fill in the blanks with words that personify. Choose appropriate words from the list provided.

| crouched whistled |
| kissed laughed |
| protected |
| danced called |
| waved smiled |

1. The sun _____ on the flowers.

2. The birds _____ a happy tune.

3. The mountain _____ the trees from the wind.

4. The bushes _____ in the howling wind.

5. The hyenas _____ at their prey.

The Amazing Helen Keller (2)

The day that Helen first recognized the meaning of the word "water" marked the most critical turning point in her life. She became a dedicated and enthusiastic learner increasing her vocabulary daily. Anne, who was experienced in teaching the Braille system of reading for blind people, taught Helen to read using this method. Her progress from this point was truly amazing.

She learned to write with a specially designed typewriter. By the age of ten, she had learned to speak and to read lips after only one month of training. At the age of twenty, she successfully completed the entrance examination to Radcliffe College. Helen graduated with honours four years later. Remarkably, she specialized in foreign languages and philosophy.

Helen's determination to make a profound contribution to the world did not stop with her personal accomplishments. She became a writer, completing her autobiography in 1903. She was determined to help the handicapped and served on the Massachusetts Commission for the Blind. Throughout her life, she was involved in fund-raising for The American Institute for the Blind. She toured England, France, Egypt, Africa, Japan, Italy, and Australia as a speaker and lecturer on behalf of the handicapped. After World War II, she visited wounded American soldiers and helped maintain morale among them.

Helen Keller completed six more books for a total of seven in all. In 1955 she wrote *Teacher: Anne Sullivan Macy*, a dedication to her teacher, Anne Sullivan. In 1959, an American author, William Gibson, wrote *The Miracle Worker*, a play about Helen's life. This play was turned into a major motion picture in 1962.

Helen Keller's story is an inspirational account of the incredible courage of a young girl.

Finding Important Information

A. Copy the exact words from the story that prove that each statement below is correct.

1. The incident with the water was very important to Helen.

   _____

   _____

2. Helen was a successful author.

   _____

   _____

3. Helen's story inspired Hollywood moviemakers.

   _____

   _____

4. Helen helped many blind and disabled people.

   _____

   _____

5. Anne knew all about teaching blind people how to read.

   _____

   _____

6. Helen was able to get a university education.

   _____

   _____

7. Helen was not only able to learn English.

   _____

   _____

8. With her work, Helen travelled outside the United States.

   _____

   _____

Building a Simple Sentence

- A simple sentence is made up of a subject, a predicate, and often descriptive words describing the subject and predicate.

  Here are a group of words that, when properly arranged, would make up a sentence that makes sense.

  Example: water / stepped / the / silly / into / child / muddy / the
  The silly child stepped into the muddy water.

  It would not make sense to say that "The muddy child stepped into the silly water". Nor would it be proper to say that "The silly water stepped into the muddy child".

B. Rearrange the following groups of words into sentences that make sense. Underline the bare predicate (verb) and circle the bare subject.

> *Keep the adjectives (words that describe nouns) and the adverbs (words that describe verbs) close to the words they are describing.*

1. store   at   the   bought   candy   children   the   the

   _____

2. racing   the   track   the   roared   cars   around

   _____

3. ice   the   careful   slipping   be   of   on

   _____

4. the   steaming   boy   pizza   hot   hungry   ate   the

   _____

5. water   colourful   drifted   the   across   sailboat   calm   the

   _____

Suffixes and Prefixes

- A Prefix is an addition to the front of a word; a Suffix is added to the end of a word. Adding a prefix or a suffix to a root word forms a new word. In some cases an opposite meaning is created. In other cases there is a change in the form of the root word.

  Examples:
  When the prefix "un" is added to "happy", the word "unhappy", which has an opposite meaning, is created.
  When the suffix "ness" is added to the word "happy", the new word "happiness" (a noun) is formed.

C. Write the root word of each of the following in the space provided.

1. inappropriate _____

2. unkind _____

3. misspelled _____

4. inability _____

5. firmness _____

6. incomplete _____

D. Create a new word for each root word by adding either a prefix or a suffix below (Some suffixes and prefixes may be used more than once).

| un | im | able | in | ous | ation | ful | dis |

1. help _____

2. possible _____

3. love _____

4. form _____

5. afraid _____

6. nerve _____

7. move _____

8. clear _____

9. agree _____

10. prove _____

11. truth _____

12. fame _____

13. crease _____

14. tend _____

Comprehension – Recalling Facts

A. Circle the letters of the correct answers.

1. The fastest member of the cat family is the
   - A. snow leopard.
   - B. cougar.
   - C. cheetah.
   - D. sabre-toothed tiger.

2. One of the following is not a member of the cat family:
   - A. lynx
   - B. lion
   - C. jaguar
   - D. weasel

3. The efforts to develop the automobile go back to the early
   - A. 1600's.
   - B. 1770's.
   - C. 1920's.
   - D. 1840's.

4. Internal combustion refers to
   - A. steam engines.
   - B. gas and air.
   - C. electric power.
   - D. front-wheel drive.

5. In 1865 a successful gas-powered car was built by
   - A. Karl Benz.
   - B. Henry Ford.
   - C. Joseph Gugnot.
   - D. Nicholas Otto.

6. The first gas-powered automobile was capable of speeds of up to
   - A. 50 mph.
   - B. 95 mph.
   - C. 9 mph.
   - D. 22 mph.

7. Cars became available to everyone because of
   - A. cheaper materials.
   - B. mass production.
   - C. better wages.
   - D. competition.

8. Ford got the idea for an assembly line from
   - A. Karl Benz.
   - B. a slaughterhouse.
   - C. a bicycle shop.
   - D. his wife.

9. The first American car for the people was the
   - A. Cadillac.
   - B. Mercedes Benz.
   - C. Model T.
   - D. Ford pick-up truck.

10. Henry Ford paid his workers the high wage of
    A. $5.00 a day.   B. $1.00 an hour.
    C. $50.00 a week.   D. $10.00 a day.

11. The number of people that died from the worldwide flu epidemic in 1919 was
    A. 50 million.   B. 5 million.   C. 25 million.   D. 100 million.

12. To fight against flu viruses, doctors invented
    A. syrups.   B. Tylenol.   C. vaccines.   D. pills.

13. Marco Polo's greatest contribution was
    A. finding a route to America.   B. writing a book about his travels.
    C. climbing the Himalayas.   D. renaming Constantinople Instanbul.

14. Christopher Columbus was sponsored by
    A. the English nobility.   B. Queen Isabella.
    C. King Henry.   D. Louis XIV.

15. Magellan was killed
    A. by pirates.   B. in the Philippines.
    C. by his own men.   D. in a storm.

16. Gypsies originated in
    A. America.   B. England.   C. India.   D. China.

17. Gypsies are becoming extinct because of
    A. disease.   B. famine.   C. assimilation. D. overcrowding.

18. Helen Keller first learned to communicate through
    A. touch.   B. sound.   C. smell.   D. hearing.

19. Helen Keller became
    A. a writer and speaker.   B. a nurse.
    C. an artist.   D. a college professor.

20. The play and the film about Keller's life was titled
    A. The Keller Story.   B. The Keller Miracle.
    C. The Miracle Worker.   D. Anne and Helen.

B. Indicate the use of the underlined pronouns by placing I (indirect object), D (direct object), or S (subject) in the spaces provided.

1. <u>She</u> wore her winter boots to school. _____

2. Ashley gave <u>him</u> the book to read. _____

3. The teacher told <u>him</u> to collect the homework. _____

4. The parents committee asked <u>her</u> to help raise funds. _____

5. The soccer ball hit <u>him</u> and a goal was prevented. _____

6. <u>They</u> were late for school. _____

7. As a joke, the boys tossed <u>him</u> into the swimming pool. _____

C. Place the correct corresponding pronouns in the spaces provided.

1. Paul brought his / its _____ dog to school.

2. She / It _____ was a cold and windy day.

3. We / They _____ warmed our hands on the radiator.

4. Sam and Peter helped we / us _____ do our / their _____ homework.

5. The players wore their / our _____ uniforms with pride.

The Sentence and Its Parts

D. Use a vertical line to divide each sentence into subject and predicate. Underline the bare subject and bare predicate (verb).

> *A basic sentence is made up of a subject and a predicate.*

1. The cat chased the dog around the yard.

2. The moon shone brightly in the night sky.

3. Happiness is skiing down a mountain.

4. The students cheered their track and field team to victory.

5. He falls down whenever he catches the ball.

Direct Object of the Verb

E. Underline the direct object in each sentence below.

1. The player kicked the ball into the net.

2. The car burned too much gas.

3. The spider trapped the fly in its web.

4. The morning dewdrops soaked the flowers.

5. The burning sun scorched his shoulders.

6. When the bell rang, the students formed a straight line.

An object is the receiver of the action of the verb.

Descriptive Language

F. Underline the adjectives and place parentheses ( ) around the adverbs in the following passage.

It was a cold and windy winter morning. The frozen streets were dangerously slippery. The delivery truck moved slowly down the icy street stopping cautiously in front of the grocery store. The driver stepped gently onto the sidewalk and held the car door tightly, cleverly avoiding a slip on the first step.

Building Sentences

Find the suitable subject and verb first and then build your sentence.

G. Using your knowledge of sentence structure, create proper sentences by rearranging the words given.

1. inside   the   for   shelter   rain   he   stop   to   the   waited

_____

2. sports   his   soccer   favourite   were   hockey   and

_____

3. five she old skating years when joined she just was the club

_____

4. blue was calm water sky was the and the

_____

5. day school were awards the given on out last of

_____

Recalling New Words

H. Match the words from the reading passages of Units 1 – 9 with the synonyms.

NEW WORDS FROM READING PASSAGES

extinct	domestic	stalk	critical	unsuspecting
inspired	excursion	objective	exotic	broad

SYNONYMS

1. spacious _____

2. non-existent _____

3. hunt _____

4. unusual _____

5. serious _____

6. tame _____

7. trip _____

8. purpose _____

9. encouraged _____

10. innocent _____

Descriptive Language

I.   **Choose a more vivid descriptive word from the word bank below that has the same meaning as each word in the list.**

exit	hazardous	scurried	fluffy	depart	towering	firm
stroll	strike	enormous	attractive	agreeable	extensive	swift

1. big _____

2. pretty _____

3. nice _____

4. fast _____

5. long _____

6. high _____

7. unsafe _____

8. soft _____

9. hard _____

10. leave _____

11. go _____

12. walk _____

13. ran _____

14. hit _____

Composing Descriptive Sentences

J.   **Add an adjective and adverb from the word bank below to each sentence to create more interesting sentences.**

cheerfully	loudly	swiftly	athletic
ferocious	speedy	angry	vicious	happy

1. The dog barked.

   _____

2. The girls ran.

   _____

3. The crowd yelled.

   _____

Who Is the Greatest Hockey Player of All Time?

With the retirement of Wayne Gretzky in 1999, there has been much speculation about who the greatest hockey player of all time is. Some believe this honour belongs to Gordie Howe, the great Detroit Red Wing player of the 1950's and 1960's. However, most hockey fans furiously debate between Wayne Gretzky and Bobby Orr.

Not only did Bobby Orr break all the scoring records for a defenseman, he actually changed the way the game was played. Traditionally, before Orr's time, defensemen were big, slow players who seldom attacked the goal and only occasionally had a shot on goal. Their prime function was to defend their goal and move the puck up to the forwards. Bobby Orr changed all that with his exciting end-to-end rushes.

Orr was first spotted by scouts when he was just twelve years old. By the time he reached fifteen, he was distinguishing himself amongst twenty-year-olds in one of the premier Canadian junior leagues. In 1966, his first year in the NHL, he won the Calder Trophy as a rookie of the year. He went on to become the first player ever to win four awards in one season – the MVP, the leading point scorer, the best defenseman, and the play-off MVP. He was also the first defenseman to score 100 points in a season.

Plagued by knee problems, Orr played only 10 regular season games in 1975 but managed to play for Team Canada in 1976, and he was named the tournament MVP. By the 1978 season, Orr had undergone ten knee operations with no successful results, forcing him to retire at the ripe age of thirty. One can only speculate as to what milestones Orr would have reached had he been able to continue to play.

Recalling Facts

A. Recall facts from the reading passage and answer each of the following questions in your own words.

Try to answer the questions first without looking back to the story. If you have difficulty, read over the questions and read the story again.

1. Besides Orr, name the other two great players that many people regard as the greatest hockey players of all time.

   a. _____   b. _____

2. What made Bobby Orr a different kind of defenseman?

   _____

3. What four awards did Orr win in a single season?

   a. _____   b. _____

   c. _____   d. _____

4. Why did Orr have to quit hockey so early?

   _____

5. What was his personal accomplishment on Team Canada in 1976?

   _____

6. How did Orr change the way the game was played?

   _____

   _____

Your Opinion

B. List the qualities that all great athletes in general possess that set them apart from other players.

a. _____   b. _____   c. _____

d. _____   e. _____   f. _____

Prepositions and Phrases

- A Preposition shows the connection between a noun or pronoun to other words in a sentence. Prepositions help to build phrases — groups of words that help us better understand the meaning of a sentence.

  Some common prepositions are: in, under, around, between, among, for, at, over, with, behind, into, and of.

- A Phrase can be adjective or adverb in nature. That is, it can describe a noun or the action of a verb. When it describes the action of a verb, it often answers the questions where or when.

  Example: The girls of St. Peter's School sang a song in the auditorium.

  Note the prepositions "of" and "in". Each of them introduces a phrase.
  The phrase "of St. Peter's School" describes the girls — it tells which girls they were. Since "girls" is a noun, subject of the sentence, then "of the girls" must be an adjective phrase.
  The phrase "in the auditorium" tells where the singing (verb) was done. Therefore it is an adverb phrase.

C. Place Adj. (adjective) or Adv. (adverb) in the space provided to identify the phrases underlined. Circle the preposition in each phrase.

1. <u>In the morning</u>, he walked to school alone. _____

2. <u>At night</u>, the house was scary. _____

3. The "Bells <u>of St. Mary's</u>" is a favourite Christmas movie. _____

4. The children <u>in the daycare</u> were asleep on their cots. _____

5. He was told to place his books <u>in his desk</u>. _____

6. <u>At sunrise</u>, they will go fishing. _____

7. He hid <u>under the bed</u> and didn't get found. _____

8. The treats were divided <u>among the classmates</u>. _____

9. He played hockey in his backyard <u>without lights</u>. _____

10. <u>On the coffee table</u> sat a vase of flowers and some photos. _____

Building Vocabulary – Forming New Words

D. Change the word in parentheses to a suitable form to fit the sense of the sentence.

Example: The boy was (run) _____ to catch the school bus.
In this case "running" is the suitable form.

1. The children were (give) _____ gifts at Christmas.

2. They made a (decide) _____ by checking the facts.

3. He felt (fortune) _____ to have so many friends.

4. The puppy was (love) _____.

5. The (create) _____ person was an artist.

6. The accident was caused by (careless) _____.

7. The tap stopped dripping when the faucet was (tight) _____.

8. For Math homework, they were asked to do (multiply) _____ and (divide) _____.

9. The boy was told to make himself (use) _____.

10. She was very (help) _____ to her mother.

E. The following are root words for words from the reading passage. Write the full words from the passage in the spaces below.

score	tradition	occasion	belief	distinguish	mile
him	furious	speculate	operate	success	excite

_____   _____   _____

_____   _____   _____

_____   _____   _____

Bicycles, Then and Now

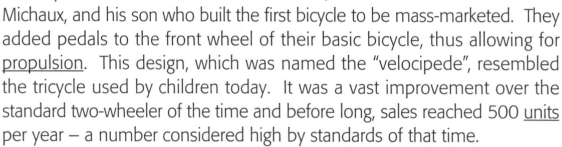

The modern bicycle is light, fast, <u>durable</u>, <u>comfortable</u>, and well-equipped, such as the models used in the world's most <u>famous</u> bike race – the Tour de France. Original bicycles, however, were very simple mechanical devices.

The first bicycles appeared in the early 19th century. It was a Frenchman from Paris, Pierre Michaux, and his son who built the first bicycle to be mass-marketed. They added pedals to the front wheel of their basic bicycle, thus allowing for <u>propulsion</u>. This design, which was named the "velocipede", resembled the tricycle used by children today. It was a vast improvement over the standard two-wheeler of the time and before long, sales reached 500 <u>units</u> per year – a number considered high by standards of that time.

The next advancement was to make the front wheels larger to improve speed. In 1887 the "safety" bicycle was designed to address <u>safety</u> issues by reducing the size of the front wheel. This model introduced the use of the chain which, when attached by two chainwheels, rotated the back wheel instead of the front. This mechanical principle of volition was based on the ratio between the number of teeth of the front chainwheel to those on the back sprocket. If, for example, the front chainwheel had 32 teeth and the rear sprocket 8, then the ratio would be 32:8; this meant that for every rotation of the front cogwheel, there were four <u>rotations</u> of the rear one, a ratio of 4 to 1. Consequently, the bicycle could have wheels of equal measure and actually increase speed.

One of the most important advancements of the safety bicycle was the addition of gears. This allowed for the use of <u>different</u> gears for particular situations. A "derailer" would shift the chain from one sprocket to another creating a new pairing of chainwheels with different ratios of teeth, and therefore, various <u>levels</u> of pedaling difficulty.

As a result of pollution and environmental concerns, there has been <u>renewed</u> interest in biking in cities worldwide.

Matching Details

A. Match the facts by drawing lines from column A to column B.

Column A	Column B
safety bicycle	home of Michaux
modern bicycle	resembled a tricycle
international race	safety bicycle was designed
Paris	ratio of gears
velocipede	first real bicycles appeared
1887	reason for today's use
32 teeth	shifts the chain
8 teeth	units sold per year
4 to 1	Tour de France
environmental concerns	front chainwheel
derailer	smaller front wheel
500	fast, durable, comfortable
19th century	rear chainwheel

 Your Opinion

B. In your opinion, give reasons for cycling to be so popular today.

1. _____ 2. _____

3. _____ 4. _____

Subordinate Clauses

- *A Subordinate Clause is like a phrase because it begins with a preposition. The clause differs from a phrase because it has a subject and a verb within it.*
  Note the difference between a phrase and a clause.
  Phrase: in the desk drawer
  Clause: whenever he came home late

  The phrase has a noun within following the preposition "in" but it does not have a verb. The clause has a pronoun (he) and a verb (came).

- *The word that introduces a clause and connects it to the principal clause, also known as the main sentence, is referred to as a subordinate conjunction. Here are examples of common subordinate conjunctions: as, if, as if, because, where, wherever, after, as long as, even if, although, since, before, whenever, while, unless, so that.*

C. Place parentheses ( ) around the subordinate clause in each of the following sentences.

1. Whenever I run too fast, my legs ache.

2. After we played the game, we ordered pizza.

3. The police arrived quickly because it was an emergency.

4. He knew he could stay as long as he wanted.

5. Even if they tried harder, they could not have won the game.

6. She rode off on her bike as the sun set.

7. He acted as if no one could see what he was doing.

8. Although the students were well-behaved, they stayed in for recess.

9. She watched television while she waited for her friend to call.

10. He knew that even if he tried, he could not forget what happened.

11. Can you tell me where he has gone for lunch?

12. I don't know what happened since I wasn't there.

13. The UFO disappeared before I could take a photo of it.

Antonyms and Synonyms

- An Antonym is an opposite meaning of a word while a Synonym is the same meaning of a word.

D. Read the clues and complete the words. They are the underlined words in the reading passage.

1. well-known (synonym)

   [ ] [A] [ ] [U] [ ]

2. danger (antonym)

   [ ] [A] [ ] [T] [ ]

3. forward motion (synonym)

   [ ] [R] [P] [ ] [ ] [ ] [O] [ ]

4. segments (synonym)

   [ ] [ ] [ ] [T] [ ]

5. similar (antonym)

   [ ] [I] [ ] [F] [ ] [R] [ ] [ ] [ ]

6. old (antonym)

   [ ] [E] [ ] [E] [ ] [E] [ ]

7. turns (synonym)

   [ ] [O] [ ] [A] [ ] [I] [ ] [ ]

8. cozy (synonym)

   [ ] [ ] [M] [ ] [O] [ ] [T] [ ] [ ] [L] [ ]

9. stages (synonym)

   [ ] [ ] [V] [ ] [L] [ ]

10. weak (antonym)

    [ ] [ ] [R] [ ] [ ] [L] [ ]

Marilyn Bell – Marathon Swimmer (1)

On September 9, 1954, 100,000 enthusiastic people waited by the Lake Ontario shore at the Canadian National Exhibition (CNE). They were there to greet a relatively unknown 16-year-old girl, Marilyn Bell, whom they hoped to see emerge from the water after her swim across Lake Ontario. By approximately 8:00 p.m., a tiny speck appeared on the water close to the shore. The crowd cheered wildly, for Miss Bell was about to do what no man or woman had accomplished before – conquer Lake Ontario.

It took Marilyn 21 hours of continuous swimming in the chilly, sometimes rough, Lake Ontario waters. Overnight she had become Canada's most famous female athlete since the great figure skater, Barbara Ann Scott. Bell's historic quest captured the hearts and minds of Canadians across the country.

Marathon swimming is a sport of personal challenge where an athlete pits himself or herself against insurmountable odds. Although very young, Marilyn was not an inexperienced long distance swimmer. She had been a member of the Lakeshore Swimming Club and had trained under the well-known swim coach, Gus Ryder. Marilyn had competed in many races, and just eight weeks before the Lake Ontario swim, she swam the Atlantic City marathon, a gruelling 20-mile race in the ocean. She spent a total of 10 hours in the water and finished two hours ahead of the nearest female competitor and came seventh overall out of forty swimmers.

This Lake Ontario marathon crossing was sponsored by the CNE. However, Marilyn was not officially invited to take part. The CNE had invited American swimmer, Florence Chadwick, to attempt the crossing and offered her a $10,000 prize upon completion. Marilyn was joined by Winnie Leuszler as unpaid and uninvited participants.

Fact or Opinion

A. Place "F" for fact or "O" for opinion beside each statement.

1. _____ The spectators went wild when Bell arrived at the CNE.

2. _____ It took Bell 21 hours to cross Lake Ontario.

3. _____ Marathon swimming is about personal challenge.

4. _____ The CNE sponsored the marathon swim.

5. _____ Florence Chadwick was offered a lot of money to participate.

6. _____ Bell was not invited to swim.

7. _____ Swimming in the lake was not a pleasant experience.

8. _____ Bell became one of Canada's greatest female athletes.

9. _____ Marilyn was not new to marathon swimming.

10. _____ Lake Ontario can be treacherous.

11. _____ Bell did fairly well in the Atlantic City marathon.

12. _____ 100,000 people came to cheer her on.

Facts are based on the exact information from the passage. Opinion is your personal view based on the facts from the reading passage.

Your Opinion

B. Give your opinion to the following questions.

1. Why was Marilyn Bell's marathon swim considered such a heroic event?

   _____

   _____

   _____

2. Do you think it was fair that Marilyn Bell was not invited to swim and not offered any money?

   _____

   _____

   _____

Building Sentences with Phrases and Clauses

- Phrases and clauses can be added to a sentence to make it more interesting.

  Example: The players on _____ were excited because _____ .

  The word "on" is a preposition used to introduce a phrase and the word "because" is a subordinate conjunction used to introduce a clause.

  You might have added the following phrase and clause to the sample sentence above:
  The players on <u>the winning team</u> were excited because <u>they won the championship</u>.

C. **Make up new sentences by adding your own phrases and clauses for the sentences below.**

Be creative!

1. Whenever _____, she is happy.

2. The key in _____ was stuck

   because _____ .

3. The horses of _____ stopped

   running when _____ .

4. The gift in _____ was hidden

   until _____ .

5. Because _____, he had to go

   to sleep in _____ .

6. He sat in _____ and waited

   while _____ .

7. Before _____, he was the best

   hockey player on _____ .

Writing Descriptions

D. **The topics below are related to the passage "Marilyn Bell – Marathon Swimmer (1)". Create one or two descriptive sentences for each topic.**

Use any or all of the descriptive words provided with each topic to add detail to your sentences. Change these words to suit the use in your sentences. Use a dictionary to look up the meanings of words that are unfamiliar to you.

1. The waters of Lake Ontario

   | choppy chilly rough battling vast waves dark struggling |

   _____

   _____

   _____

2. The crowd of people waiting at the CNE

   | anxious expectant cheering surprised excited clapping |

   _____

   _____

   _____

3. Marilyn Bell emerges from Lake Ontario

   | chilled exhausted staggering jubilant ecstatic proudly |

   _____

   _____

   _____

Marilyn Bell – Marathon Swimmer (2)

Marilyn knew that she was an unwelcome participant in the Lake Ontario challenge swim. She felt that since it was a Canadian sponsored event, a Canadian swimmer should take part. Marilyn later confessed that she was not sure that she could make it herself, but she was also unsure that Chadwick could make it. On September 8, 1954, the swimmers stepped into the chilly, 21°C Lake Ontario water at Youngstown, New York. Bell was swimming for Canada and the much-anticipated race was on!

It didn't take long for Marilyn to show her strength. Five kilometres from the American shore, she had overtaken Chadwick, and by 6:00 a.m., Chadwick had been pulled from the water after 26 km. Leuszler quit at the 32 km mark, leaving Bell as the only competitor.

The swimming conditions were less than ideal. It rained through the night and the water temperature dropped to 16°C. The water was choppy but Bell managed to maintain a steady 60 strokes a minute, for a two-mile-an-hour pace. Her biggest difficulty was boredom. On more than one occasion, Marilyn fell asleep and her coach, Gus Ryder, had to wake her up. She was fed baby food and syrup on a stick alongside the boat.

On the Canadian side, the radio stations had been broadcasting her progress and thousands of extra newspapers were being printed to meet the public demand for this incredible story. When she completed the 51.5 km swim and sat in an ambulance recovering, she exclaimed that she felt terrific. The CNE gave Bell the prize money and she received another $50,000 worth of gifts. She became an instant celebrity and a national treasure.

Marilyn Bell went on to conquer the English Channel the following year and attempted the treacherous Straits of Juan de Fuca. She failed to complete the Juan de Fuca swim but two weeks later, she covered her skin with Vaseline to offset the cold, and successfully completed the swim.

Marilyn Bell retired from marathon swimming at the age of eighteen, much to the disappointment of her fans.

Recalling Information

A. Indicate whether each statement is true or false by inserting "T" for true and "F" for false in the space provided.

1. _____ Marilyn was swimming for Canada.

2. _____ Lake Ontario was a warm 32°C the day of the swim.

3. _____ Bell's pace was 60 strokes per minute.

4. _____ Bell passed Chadwick after only 5 km into the swim.

5. _____ The race began at the CNE.

6. _____ Bell received no money but only prizes for her effort.

7. _____ Bell never swam again after her Lake Ontario victory.

8. _____ Bell fell asleep during her race.

9. _____ Bell ate syrup from a stick.

10. _____ Chadwick finished the race in second place.

11. _____ Swimming Lake Ontario was boring for Bell.

12. _____ The distance across the lake was 51.5 km.

Your Opinion

B. Answer the questions with your own opinion.

1. Why do you think Marilyn Bell retired from swimming at the age of eighteen when her best years were still ahead?

   _____

   _____

2. How did Gus Ryder, her coach, help her by being alongside her throughout the swim?

   _____

   _____

Rules of Capitalization

1. *Capitalize the first word in a sentence.*

2. *Capitalize all proper nouns that name individuals, places, and organizations, but not "the" or "of".*

3. *Capitalize titles when they come before a person's name.*

4. *Capitalize all government titles, but not "the" or "of".*

5. *Capitalize the first word of a quotation.*

6. *Capitalize points on the compass only when they are used as a distinct part of the country, i.e. the North, but not "he went north".*

C. Capitalize the words that should be capitalized.

Write directly on top of the letters you are changing. The number after the sentence tells you the number of capital letters in that sentence.

1. the injured man called for dr. smith to come to his aid. (3)

2. before their trip to london, england, mr. and mrs. anderson called the department of immigration to get their documents. (8)

3. the earl of sandwich became famous for his invention of the sandwich. (3)

4. lisa moore attended the university of toronto and received a degree in english. (5)

5. she asked, "what time will professor higgins give his speech about pioneers of the wild west?" (7)

6. although they were both canadians, james came from the west and joan came from the east, so they decided to meet in winnipeg. (7)

7. the japanese family arrived in new york on american airlines and stayed at the hilton hotel in upper manhattan. (9)

8. the mona lisa is one of da vinci's most famous paintings. (4)

Creative Writing – Composing an Interview

D. Write the questions that you will ask Ms. Bell about her heroic swim.

Pretend you are a newspaper reporter and the date is September 9, 1954. You have been waiting for Ms. Bell to emerge from Lake Ontario because you have been granted an exclusive interview. Use the facts you have learned from the reading passages (parts 1 & 2) to help make up your questions.

First question:

_____

_____

Second question:

_____

_____

Third question:

_____

_____

Fourth question:

_____

_____

Your Opinion

E. Write your opinion for the question – do you think Marilyn Bell was a hero? Write a detailed sentence to explain your answer.

_____

_____

Meat-Eating Plants

Plants are bright colourful adornments of nature that feed on sunlight and water. Or so we think. Many plants are, in fact, carnivorous. Science fiction movies have frightened us with horror stories of man-eating plants that swallow human beings whole. This notion may seem absurd to us, but it is an ugly truth for many an unsuspecting insect.

Some species of plants require the meat of an insect as a dietary supplement. There are two types of meat-eating plants. Some plants such as the Venus Flytrap actually move to capture their prey. Other plants sit and wait and let the insects trap themselves. The Sticky Sundew is covered with sticky hairs that produce a type of glue that sticks to the unsuspecting insect when it lands. The hairs then close over it and it is absorbed into the plant. The Cobra Lily, named for its snake-like appearance, lures insects by its nectar. Once an insect enters the plant, it becomes confused by the light shining through the leaves. Following this light to escape, it becomes exhausted and drops into the liquid of the plant.

The best known predator plant is the Venus Flytrap. Insects are attracted by the unusual leaf tips and cannot resist landing on them. Adding to this lure is the promise of food from sweet smelling nectar. After the insect alights on the surface of the leaf, two kidney-shaped lobes, triggered by sensitive bristles at the top of the leaf, snap shut. After about half an hour, the Venus Flytrap will secrete enzymes and acids which will slowly digest the insect. Full digestion of an insect may take up to two weeks and the trap will then be prepared for another victim. When the Venus Flytrap is ready to eat again, the trap opens and the exoskeleton of the devoured insect is blown away in the wind.

Remembering Details

A. Fill in the blanks with the appropriate words from the list provided.

Venus Flytrap enzymes diet carnivorous wind insects nectar Sticky Sundew weeks confused exoskeleton

Some plants are 1._____, that is they eat meat. They feed on unsuspecting 2._____. For some plants, meat is a necessary supplement to their regular 3._____. The 4._____ actually moves to catch its prey while the 5._____ has a sticky surface that traps its catch. The Cobra Lily lures insects by its sweet smelling 6._____. Once an insect enters the Cobra Lily, it becomes 7._____ by the light and loses its way, eventually drowning in the plant's juice. The Venus Flytrap breaks down and digests an insect using 8._____ and acids. Full digestion of an insect can take up to two 9._____. The Venus Flytrap, after digesting its victim, lets the 10._____ blow away the discarded 11._____ of the insect. Once this is done, the leaves open up again ready for the next meal.

In Your Own Words

B. Suggest three titles for horror movies about killer plants.
(Be humorous if you choose)

1. _____

2. _____

3. _____

Complete EnglishSmart • **Grade 5**   65

Punctuation Rules for Sentences

- Types of Sentences

   Declarative – simply makes a statement: I walked my dog.
   Interrogative – asks a question: Did you walk your dog?
   Exclamatory – shows emotion: Help me, I'm falling!
   Imperative – gives a command without emotion: Give me that pencil.

- Using the Comma

   1. Use a comma to separate words in a series or list.
      Example: We played hockey, baseball, basketball, and tennis.

   2. Use a comma between adjectives describing a noun.
      Example: The tall, thin, poorly dressed man walked by.

   3. Use a comma to separate a noun in apposition.
      Example: My friend, Paul, came to visit me.

   4. Use a comma in dates.
      Example: Her birthday was July 22, 1953.

   5. Use a comma after long subordinate clauses that appear first.
      Example: After we ate the meal that mother prepared, we went for a walk.

   6. Use a comma to set off a direct quotation.
      Example: She asked, "May I use your telephone?"

C. Punctuate the sentences below.

The number at the end of each sentence represents the number of punctuation marks needed.

1. When Susan went shopping at the local store she bought milk bread cheese eggs and butter (6)

2. Why do certain sports such as hockey golf and tennis cost so much to play (3)

3. "Get out of bed right now or you'll be late for school" my mother yelled "Don't you realize it's September 5 the first day of school" (4)

4. Where would a person go to find good weather interesting shopping friendly people and inexpensive accommodations (4)

5. Look out the tree branch is breaking off (2)

6. Hand in your test papers your special pencils and your question sheets now (3)

7. John's father Mr. Williams carried the balls the bases and the bats (5)

Searching for Synonyms

D. Match the synonyms with the words from the passage.

> *Draw a line to pair up the words that are similar in meaning and use your dictionary to find the meanings of unfamiliar words.*

Synonym	Word from the reading passage
addition	carnivorous
lands	prey
leak	devoured
victim	nectar
dazed	supplement
food	secrete
decorations	predator
taken in	alights
hunter	dietary
strange	confused
sweet liquid	adornments
meat-eating	absorbed
eaten	unusual

 Writing Sentences

E. Use each group of words from the reading passage in a single sentence showing their meanings.

1. predator   prey   devoured   confused

_____

2. dietary   supplement   unusual   nectar

_____

15

Pirates of the Caribbean (1)

With the discovery of the new world, more specifically the Caribbean, by Christopher Columbus, trade began between North America and Europe. Although this trade was <u>profitable</u> and great wealth lay in the transport of goods from the Caribbean, it was not without problems. Rough seas were always a concern, but a greater problem was the potential attack by pirates.

The trade <u>routes</u> across the Atlantic were well-known to pirates, some of whom had been employed as sailors on trading vessels. A pirate ship, equipped with cannons and ruthless men, would pull up alongside a trading vessel, jump aboard, and take control. If the trading ship's captain or crew resisted, they would be killed. The pirates would take the goods and recruit new members to piracy from the trading vessel's <u>crew</u>. Not all pirates were kind enough to let their victims live. Some murdered the crew of the ships and left the vessels covered with dead bodies to float on the seas, serving as a message to other ships not to resist takeover if approached.

Many sailors were attracted to the <u>carefree</u> life of a pirate travelling the high seas and getting rich from the gold and jewels found on the trading vessels. After a few successful <u>raids</u>, they could <u>retire</u> to one of the <u>exotic</u> Caribbean islands or head home to their <u>native</u> land.

Not all pirates were bandits. There was a distinct group called Privateers who were actually hired by a country to pirate the trading vessels of a rival country. The British, for example, hired privateers to attack Spanish vessels. They required only 10% of the <u>booty</u> obtained from the pirated <u>vessel</u>. When England took Jamaica from the Spanish, they hired Captain Henry Morgan (the well-known face on rum bottles sold today) to protect the island by attacking Spanish ships. Morgan became wealthy from the "booty" he obtained and received favourable recognition by the English navy.

Cause and Effect

A. Place a check mark beside the correct "cause" listed for each "effect" stated.

1. Pirates were anxious to attack trading ships.

   a. ☐ The pirates wanted revenge.

   b. ☐ The ships were carrying valuable goods.

   c. ☐ The pirates were at war.

2. Pirates were familiar with the trading routes.

   a. ☐ The pirates had been sailors on trading ships.

   b. ☐ Pirates had stolen the trading route maps.

   c. ☐ The pirates were born in the Caribbean.

3. Pirates sometimes killed their victims unnecessarily.

   a. ☐ The pirates panicked when they were robbing a ship.

   b. ☐ Dead sailors warned other trading ships not to resist.

   c. ☐ Pirates do not take prisoners.

4. Many sailors wanted to be pirates.

   a. ☐ Pirates were able to travel.

   b. ☐ Pirates lived a carefree life.

   c. ☐ Sailing was hard work.

5. Not all pirates were criminals.

   a. ☐ Privateers were hired by various countries.

   b. ☐ Some pirates gave away all the goods they stole.

   c. ☐ Some pirates were kind and friendly.

6. Henry Morgan was a famous pirate.

   a. ☐ He killed many sailors.

   b. ☐ He was hired by England to protect Jamaica.

   c. ☐ He liked to drink rum.

Active Voice and Passive Voice

- In sentences written in active voice, the subject performs the action expressed in the verb; the subject acts.

  Example: The pirates would take the goods from the trading vessel.

  In sentences written in passive voice, the subject receives the action expressed in the verb; the subject is acted upon. The agent performing the action may appear in a "by the..." phrase that can sometimes be omitted.

  Example: The goods would be taken by the pirates from the trading vessel.

  Or: The goods would be taken from the trading vessel.

B. Determine whether each of the following sentences is active or passive. If it is active, change it to passive and if it is passive, change it to active.

1. The girls were given free time by the music teacher to finish the songs.

   _____

2. The girls composed the lively tune.

   _____

3. Sam and Pam made the pizza.

   _____

4. The pizza was enjoyed by the whole family.

   _____

5. They parked the car in the shade.

   _____

6. The clown gave each child a balloon.

   _____

Crossword Puzzle

C. Use the clues to fill in the crossword puzzle with the underlined words from the reading passage.

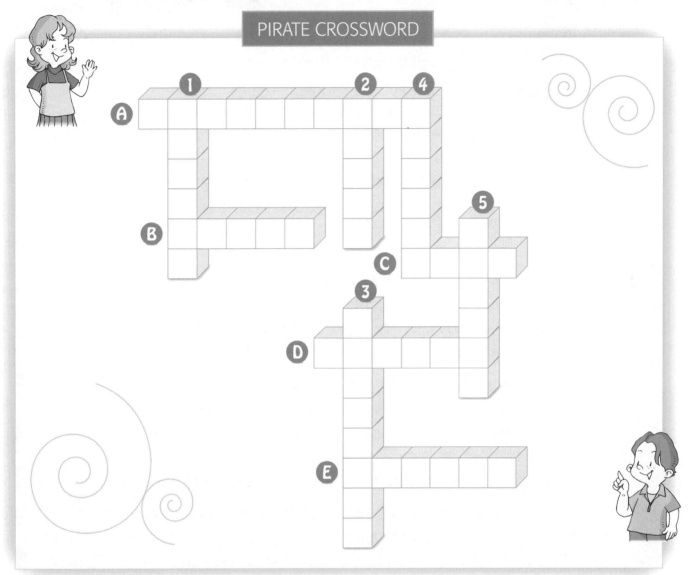

PIRATE CROSSWORD

16

Pirates of the Caribbean (2)

Pirates, such as Captain Henry Morgan, were also referred to as Buccaneers. They became legendary as stories about their ruthlessness and their skills at pirating spread throughout the Caribbean and the southern coast of North America. The most notorious pirate of them all was Edward Teach, better known as Blackbeard. He was tall and muscular with a long beard braided with bright ribbons that hung down to his chest. He was a fearful sight. When he went into battle, he would put slow burning fuses in his hair, creating a smoky haze that surrounded his head. If his opponents put up a fight, he would teach them a lesson. In one case, he cut off the nose of a Portuguese sailor; in another, he killed one of his own men just to remind his crew of how evil he was. It was acts like these that spread his reputation far and wide and made piracy easy for him.

Piracy was taking its toll on the economy of the major trading countries. Doing business in the Caribbean and the Carolina coast was becoming very expensive. The Governor of Virginia, Alexander Spotswood, put up a reward of 100 British pounds (approximately $230) for the capture of Blackbeard. This amount was roughly ten years' wages for a sailor at the time.

A British naval officer named Maynard took up the challenge with a crew of 60, and found Blackbeard hiding in a North Carolina inlet. The next day, Maynard attacked Blackbeard and on the second attack found himself face to face with Blackbeard. Maynard shot him but Blackbeard didn't fall. They then fought with swords, and just as Blackbeard was about to deliver a fatal blow, one of Maynard's crew shot and killed him.

With Blackbeard's death came the end of piracy. However, the governor refused to give Maynard the reward of 100 British pounds. Instead he gave him only 3 pounds ($7) and half that to his crew. This paltry payment was hardly worth risking their lives.

Understanding Content

A. **For each statement below, write the exact sentence or phrase from the story that supports that statement.**

1. Pirates became legends for the awful things that they did.

   _____

2. The pirates were hurting the economy of trading countries because of their thieving.

   _____

3. Edward Teach was unforgettable because of his appearance.

   _____

4. Teach sometimes performed acts of incredible cruelty.

   _____

5. Piracy was easy for Blackbeard because of his reputation.

   _____

6. Maynard, an English naval officer, went looking for Blackbeard.

   _____

7. Maynard was lucky Blackbeard didn't kill him.

   _____

8. Maynard's efforts were for nothing.

   _____

9. The death of Blackbeard changed everything.

   _____

10. It was not worth it to try to capture Blackbeard.

   _____

Verb Tenses

- A Verb Tense shows the time of the action of the verb.
- Present tense – action going on in the present

  Example: The boy runs home from school.

  Past tense – action occurred in the past

  Example: The boy ran home.
- Future tense – action will happen in the future; the verb may be accompanied by "shall" or "will"

  Example: The boy will run home.

B. Fill in the missing verb tenses in the chart below.

Although some of these have irregular tense forms, they should be familiar to you.

	PRESENT	PAST	FUTURE
1.	throw	threw	will throw
2.		bled	
3.	begin		
4.		came	
5.	do		
6.			will think
7.	fight		
8.	lose		
9.		wore	
10.	write		
11.		grew	
12.			will shake

Writing Poetry with a Rhyming Scheme

- Poems often have strict rhyming schemes that they follow throughout. Here are two sample rhyming schemes:

Example 1 – scheme	a b a b	Example 2 – scheme	a a b b
The sun was bright	a	Swinging on a tree	a
The wind was low	b	She felt happy and free	a
The bird took flight	a	Gliding up into the air	b
His wings aglow	b	Without a single care	b

In example one, the first and third lines rhyme as do the second and fourth.
In example two, the first and second lines rhyme as do the third and fourth.

- The lines grouped together with a rhyming scheme form a stanza.

The Challenge

C. Create a poem of one stanza about Pirates of the Caribbean using either of the rhyming schemes above.

Here are some rhyming pairs to help you get started. If you prefer, create your own rhyming words. You may want to use the information from the passages, Pirates of the Caribbean (1) (2), to give you ideas for your poem.

Rhyming Words

fight - might - sight	beard - feared	booty - snooty	death - breath
teach - reach limb - trim	raid - afraid	battle - rattle	mate - fate
glorious - notorious	coast - boast - most	mess - confess	aboard - sword

Title: _____

_____

_____

_____

_____

The Origins of the Written Words

By the age of six or seven, most school children around the world are able to print words and begin to create stories. By this time, they have already <u>mastered</u> speech and can <u>communicate</u> their thoughts <u>effectively</u>. Can you imagine a world without verbal and written communication? Like most things in the <u>civilized</u> world, language was part of an evolutionary <u>process</u>.

Early man, known as *Homo sapiens*, communicated by drawing pictures on the walls of caves. They would draw pictures of their hunts for food and of important <u>social</u> and personal family events. It was not until 3000 B.C. that actual writing, a method of recording language sounds, came into being. Early forms of writing were traced back to the Sumerians of Mesopotamia. Their writing was made up of <u>symbols</u> called *logograms* that stood for words or phrases. This <u>system</u> <u>evolved</u> to include representations of syllables. Thus the Sumerians were using both *logograms* and *syllabic forms* to <u>create</u> writing.

To avoid <u>confusion</u>, sounds, such as the vowel and consonant sounds that we use today, were given <u>specific</u> symbols. This was the early creation of an *alphabetic* system. There are not many symbols needed to create a language. For example, the English language uses an alphabet with only 26 letters but there are over 500,000 English words listed in the Oxford Dictionary.

The Egyptians developed *hieroglyphics*, a system of writing, approximately a hundred years after the Sumerian system. Many forms of writing were adapted by other peoples until about the year 1500 B.C. when a <u>partially</u> alphabetic system was created. This marked the early stages of writing as we know it today. The Greeks are credited with separating vowel and consonant sounds by 750 B.C., thereby creating the fully alphabetic system, which paved the way for the full development of organized language.

The Main Idea

A. Below are summary ideas for each paragraph. Place a check mark in the space provided for the summary statement that best suits each paragraph.

Paragraph One

1. _____ Language has evolved over the years.
2. _____ Children have learned how to write.
3. _____ What if the world had no communication

Paragraph Two

1. _____ Early writing was in the form of drawing.
2. _____ The roots of early language
3. _____ Homo sapiens - early man

> In each paragraph, there is a main idea that is the subject of the paragraph.

Paragraph Three

1. _____ Sounds were given symbols.
2. _____ The alphabet was created.
3. _____ A dictionary was written.

Paragraph Four

1. _____ The origins of the alphabet system for writing
2. _____ The Greeks separated vowels and consonants.
3. _____ Egyptians developed hieroglyphics.

B. Place a number from 1 – 5 beside each of the events to indicate the order in which they occurred.

☐ Hieroglyphics were created.

☐ The alphabet was created.

☐ Pictures were drawn in caves.

☐ Symbols were used for words.

☐ Sounds were given symbols.

Verb Agreement

- The verb in a sentence must agree with its subject and must change to the tense needed in the sentence.

  Example 1: We go. He goes. She goes. They go.

  Note the changes in the verb "go".

  Example 2: He is ... / She is ... / We are ... / They are ... / We are ...

  These are forms of the infinitive "to be".

C. Circle the correct noun or verb for each of the sentences below.

1. The first day of the school year is, were an exciting day.

2. We, She is the new student in the school.

3. The teacher tell, told the students about all the rules.

4. When the recess bell rang, rung , the students went, go outside.

5. Paul and John was, were the first students to get to the school yard.

6. They would play, played basketball for the entire recess.

7. When the bell rings, rung , they will came, come inside.

8. The students were sat, seated in rows.

9. One of the teachers could speak, spoke three languages.

10. After school, activities were offered, offer to the students.

11. Some would choose, chose sports. Others preferred, prefer clubs.

12. The school bus will take, took some of the pupils home at the end of the day.

13. The teacher said that homework should be doing, done regularly.

14. The students, student were not too happy about having, have homework.

Word Building Chart

D. Fill in the chart below creating new words from the "original" words taken from the passage.

Locate each word in the passage and learn its meaning from the sentence in which it appears.

ORIGINAL WORD (from passage)	NEW WORD (add prefix / suffix)	SYNONYM/ANTONYM/ DEFINITION	RHYMING WORD
mastered			
communicate			
effectively			
civilized			
process			
social			
symbols			
system			
evolved			
create			
confusion			
specific			
partially			

PROGRESS TEST 2

Recalling Details

A. Place a check mark beside the best answer to complete each statement.

1.   One of Bobby Orr's accomplishments was that

  a. ☐ he was better than Wayne Gretsky.

  b. ☐ he was the first player to win four awards in one season.

  c. ☐ he played for Team Canada.

2.   Orr retired early because

  a. ☐ he wanted to start a business.

  b. ☐ he was too old to play any longer.

  c. ☐ his knee was too damaged.

3.   The most famous bike race in the world is

  a. ☐ the Tour de France.

  b. ☐ the American Cross Country Race.

  c. ☐ the Ride Across Europe.

4.   The most important development of the safety bicycle was

  a. ☐ creating a larger front wheel.

  b. ☐ the addition of gears.

  c. ☐ creating a smaller front wheel.

5.   Marilyn Bell finished her Lake Ontario swim at

  a. ☐ City Hall.

  b. ☐ the CNE.

  c. ☐ Toronto Harbour.

6.   Just eight weeks before the Lake Ontario swim, Bell swam the

  a. ☐ Pacific Ocean Marathon.

  b. ☐ English Channel.

  c. ☐ Atlantic City Marathon.

7. Marilyn Bell swam across Lake Ontario from
   a. [ ] Youngstown to Toronto.
   b. [ ] Toronto to Youngstown.
   c. [ ] Buffalo to Toronto.

8. Bell's reward for her heroic effort was
   a. [ ] $50,000 in prizes.
   b. [ ] $10,000 award from the CNE.
   c. [ ] $50,000 in gifts and $10,000 from CNE.

9. Meat-eating plants like to devour
   a. [ ] small animals.
   b. [ ] human beings.
   c. [ ] insects.

10. Sailors were easily recruited as pirates because they
    a. [ ] enjoyed stealing and torturing people.
    b. [ ] liked the idea of travelling the high seas and getting rich.
    c. [ ] wanted to stop vessels from trading with other countries.

11. Not all pirates were actual bandits. Some were
    a. [ ] hired by some countries to attack the vessels of rival countries.
    b. [ ] secret agents out to capture other pirates.
    c. [ ] lost at sea.

12. Blackbeard was the most feared pirate because
    a. [ ] he was small but fearless.
    b. [ ] he was cunning and hard to catch.
    c. [ ] he performed acts of cruelty as a warning to sailors.

13. The earliest form of written communication was
    a. [ ] hieroglyphics.
    b. [ ] cave drawings.
    c. [ ] alphabetic system.

Building Sentences with Subordinate Clauses and Descriptive Phrases

B. **Here are various subordinate clauses. Create statements to finish the sentences.**

1. When the students hear the recess bell,

   _____

2. After they ate their lunch,

   _____

3. Whenever his uncle comes to visit,

   _____

4. The children were surprised when

   _____

C. **Create adverb and adjective phrases that complete the following sentences.**

1. The players on _____ arrived at _____ for their _____ against _____.

2. In _____ Grandma found her old photo album from _____.

3. At _____ it was time to get on _____ and head home for _____.

4. In _____ he woke up and pulled his clothes from _____ and put his books in _____.

Sentence Punctuation and Capitalization

D. Punctuate each of the sentences below.

Recall the rules of capitalization given in Unit 13 and the examples of sentence punctuation given in Unit 14.

1. is it cold outside she asked

2. sams birthday was august 15 1989

3. stop don't move screamed the police officer

4. dr smith worked for the canadian ministry of health

5. the small frightened siamese cat curled up in her lap

6. on a recent trip to montreal his family went to watch the expos

7. why do canadians enjoy hockey so much especially the toronto maple leafs

8. one day he hoped to play basketball in the nba but first he would have to grow much taller

Verb Agreement

E. Choose the proper word to match the sense and tense of each sentence.

1. The boys was, were _____ waiting for the girls to finish, finished _____ using the baseball diamond.

2. Susan and Debbie tells, tell _____ a story to the small children.

3. Ice-cream and cake were, was _____offered at the party.

4. The adults views, viewed _____ a movie while the children played, plays _____ games.

5. When the bus come, came _____, the students line, lined _____ up to take, took _____ a seat.

6. The teacher was, were _____ pleased with the behaviour of the students who went, go _____ on the school trip.

7. Skiing and skating is, are _____ two sports that require, requires _____ balance.

F.   Make changes to the words in parentheses to suit the sentences. Be careful of verb tense, subject-verb agreement, and part of speech.

Example:	John (fly) _____ in a small airplane last week.
	You would change "fly" to "flew" to suit the verb tense.

1.   He was (run) _____ when he tripped and fell.

2.   The sun (rise) _____ in the East and (set) _____ in the West every day.

3.   He was (satisfy) _____ to have finished second in the race.

4.   The school work was not (complete) _____ on time.

5.   The company slogan read, "Satisfaction (guarantee) _____."

6.   The (replace) _____ top on the bottle was convenient.

7.   He couldn't tell the (different) _____ between the twins.

8.   He ran (swift) _____ and (defeat) _____ the leading (run) _____ in the race.

9.   She (sew) _____ a button on her sweater after she had (wash) _____ and (hang) _____ it out to dry.

10. The winter storm (sweep) _____ across the town overnight, (cover) _____ all the houses with snow.

G.   Change the following words to the past tense.

1.	fly	_____	2.	know	_____
3.	go	_____	4.	think	_____
5.	buy	_____	6.	build	_____
7.	do	_____	8.	try	_____
9.	is	_____	10.	throw	_____

H. Fill in the blanks in the puzzle pairs using both the clues and the words listed below.

PUZZLE WORDS TO MATCH THE CLUES

evolved	propulsion	create	process	furious	speculate
excite	social	mastered	durable	predator	distinguish

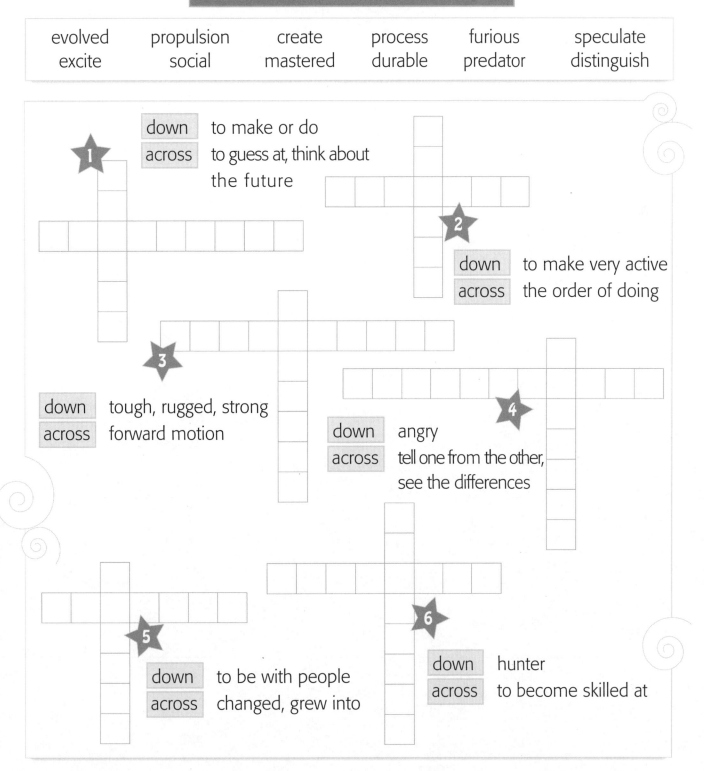

1
down — to make or do
across — to guess at, think about the future

2
down — to make very active
across — the order of doing

3
down — tough, rugged, strong
across — forward motion

4
down — angry
across — tell one from the other, see the differences

5
down — to be with people
across — changed, grew into

6
down — hunter
across — to become skilled at

Grammar

1 Nouns and Noun Use

A **Compound Noun** is formed when two or more words are put together.
Examples: flashlight, fireplace

A **Collective Noun** represents a group of persons, places, or things.
Examples: audience, crowd, crew

Exercise A

In the space provided at the end of each sentence, state whether the underlined noun is simple, proper, compound, or collective.

> Do you remember what simple or proper nouns are?

1. The <u>band</u> played a marching tune. _____
2. <u>Dr. Parker</u> visited his patients in the hospital. _____
3. The <u>sheep</u> grazed in the meadow. _____
4. The <u>child</u> enjoyed an ice cream cone. _____
5. The <u>firemen</u> were able to put out the burning blaze. _____
6. The bowl was filled with a <u>bunch</u> of grapes. _____
7. The <u>pack</u> of wolves lived together. _____
8. The new automobile had all the latest safety <u>features</u>. _____
9. Professor Atkinson worked at the <u>University of Toronto</u>. _____
10. He tied his <u>shoelace</u> tighter. _____
11. The boys finally won the <u>game</u>. _____
12. Please put the <u>pile</u> of paper into the drawer. _____

> Let's now look more closely at compound nouns.

Compound Nouns can be formed in three ways:
1. joining two nouns together to form one word
2. placing two words next to each other without joining them
3. using a hyphen to link two or more words

Exercise B

Underline the compound nouns in the following sentences.

> There are 16 compound nouns in the 10 sentences below.

1. My father's brother-in-law was a fireman.

2. In our classroom, we had a tomato plant on the window sill.

3. My parents pay fire insurance on our home.

4. In his bedroom he has a fireplace.

5. When you get into a car, be sure to put on your seat belt.

6. Always keep a flashlight in the trunk of the car.

7. When she is older, she is going to be a baby-sitter.

8. After grade eight, we will attend high school.

9. He wants to get a motorcycle when he is old enough to drive.

10. She is the great-grandchild of her mother's grandmother.

Collective Nouns represent groups of people or things.

Example: The crew is busy preparing for the launch of the new ocean liner.
The word "crew" is a collective noun referring to all the people working on the ocean liner.

Exercise C

Underline the collective noun in each group of nouns below.

> Remember: A collective noun may look like a singular noun but it represents a group of things or people.

1. flock birds

2. army soldiers

3. sailors navy

4. person group

5. fan audience

6. witness jury

7. father mother family

8. singer orchestra

9. people crowd

10. player team

11. students class

12. member committee

Verb Agreement

When a collective noun is used as a subject of a sentence, it will have either a singular or plural verb depending on the meaning of the sentence.

Example (1): The crowd cheers the winner of the race.
In this case, the collective noun "crowd" is referred to as a single unit and requires the singular form of the verb "cheer" which is "cheers".

Example (2): The family like to read books together.
In this case, the collective noun "family" represents the individuals within the family and the verb must therefore be plural.

Exercise D

Select the correct verb to suit the meaning of the collective noun in each of the following sentences.

Read each sentence carefully to see whether the meaning involves the individual members of the group or whether it refers to the group as a single unit.

1. The army _____ (protect, protects) the citizens of the country.

2. The army _____ (visit, visits) their family whenever they can.

3. The team _____ (play, plays) many games in a season.

4. The team _____ (chooses, choose) their own personal equipment.

5. The audience _____ (applaud, applauds) the performance.

6. The audience _____ (finds, find) their seats before the performance begins.

7. The family _____ (eats, eat) dinner together.

8. The family _____ (go, goes) home at different times after dinner.

Noun Plurals

To form the plurals of simple nouns, apply the following rules:

1. in many cases, just add "**s**".
2. if a noun ends in "s", "x", "ch", or "sh", add "**es**".
3. if a noun ends in "o", and there is a vowel before the "o", add "**s**".
4. if a noun ends in "o", and there is a consonant before the "o", add "**es**".
5. if a noun ends in "y", and a vowel comes before the "y", add "**s**".
6. if a noun ends in "y", and a consonant comes before the "y", change the "y" to "i" and add "**es**".
7. if the noun ends in "f" or "fe", change the "f" to "v", and add "**es**".

Exercise E

Refer to the rules and make plurals of the singular nouns below. Place the plural words and the rule numbers in the spaces provided.

Singular	Plural	Number
1. ship	_____	_____
2. knife	_____	_____
3. hero	_____	_____
4. country	_____	_____
5. cowboy	_____	_____
6. bush	_____	_____
7. zoo	_____	_____

Changing Verbs to Nouns

Nouns can be created from verbs.

Example: "**Play**" is a verb and "**player**" is a noun formed from the verb.

Exercise F

From each of the verbs below, create a suitable noun.

1. sing _____
2. run _____
3. dance _____
4. swim _____
5. hike _____
6. teach _____
7. bake _____
8. climb _____
9. drive _____
10. work _____

CHALLENGE

Can you create the noun for each of the following?

1. One who creates art is an _____ .

2. A person who types is a _____ .

3. A person who specializes in mathematics is a _____ .

4. A writer of books is also known as an _____ .

2 Pronouns

Types of Pronouns

A pronoun functions as a noun in a sentence. Often, a pronoun takes the place of a specific noun in a sentence or previous sentence in a paragraph. The noun that a pronoun replaces is called an "antecedent". A pronoun must agree in number and gender with its antecedent.

Example (1): The train was late because **it** had many stops to make.
The pronoun "it" refers to its antecedent noun "train".

Example (2): Susan left the book in the classroom as **she** didn't have time to read it.
The pronoun "she" agrees in gender (female) and number (singular) with "Susan".

Exercise A

In each of the following sentences, circle the proper pronoun.

1. The boys played baseball during recess; (he   she   they) finished the game just as the bell rang.

2. Paul and Richard were late for school because (he   they   it) missed the bus.

3. I will be forever grateful to my teacher who helped (me   I   my) improve my reading skills.

4. The students enjoy creating artwork after they finish (their   our   your) other work.

5. The bell will ring in the schoolyard but we may not hear (them   it   those).

6. In the summer, Eric and Josh will go to the cottage where (we   they   he) will have lots of fun.

Demonstrative Pronouns

These pronouns identify specific nouns.

Examples: **This** is my desk.   **Those** are his books.
That is my classroom.

> Using a demonstrative pronoun is like pointing to something by using language.

Interrogative Pronouns

These pronouns ask a question.

Examples: **Where** is my lunch box?
Which of these hats is yours?

Exercise B

Put suitable demonstrative or interrogative pronouns in the following sentences.

1. This is my coat, but _____ one is his?

2. _____ one of my friends should I invite to the Blue Jay game?

3. _____ is your school located?

4. You like that one but I would rather use _____ one.

5. _____ are the best skis. They are even better than these.

6. _____ will you arrive and _____ direction will you be coming from?

7. _____ will be attending the meeting and _____ will it be held?

8. _____ will we be in 20 years? _____ is a tricky question.

A **Relative Pronoun** relates a dependent clause (one that does not stand alone) to the rest of the sentence.

Example: This is the new car **which** my father bought today.

The relative pronoun "which" connects the dependent clause "which my father bought today" to the rest of the sentence.

Rules: 1. use "who" when relating to people
2. use "which" when referring to other living creatures and to things
3. use "that" for either persons or things

Exercise C

Refer to the rules above and place the proper relative pronoun in each of the following sentences.

1. Sara was wearing the new sweater _____ she received as a birthday gift.

2. The tree _____ was in the backyard was the tallest in the neighbourhood.

3. His uncle _____ was visiting from Vancouver stayed for two weeks.

4. He chose to volunteer for the charity _____ helped the homeless.

5. Jenny was the one _____ did not show up.

6. The car _____ is parked on the driveway belongs to Uncle Bob.

7. Don't touch the vase _____ Mrs. Kennedy put on the coffee table.

8. The boy _____ hit three homeruns is Keith.

A **Reflex Pronoun** refers to its subject.

Example: She helped **herself** to some cake.

Exercise D

Put the proper reflex pronoun in the space provided in each of the following sentences.

1. We asked _____ whether or not we should have made the trip.

2. He pushed _____ to the limit and won the race.

3. The Maple Leafs prepared _____ for the big game.

4. We surprised _____ when we were so successful on our English test.

5. My dog hurt _____ when it tried to jump over the fence.

Do not use a reflex pronoun in place of a subject or object in a sentence.

CHALLENGE

In 5 of the following sentences, there is a misused reflexive pronoun. Cross it out and replace it with a proper pronoun.

1. You may call John or myself for the information.   _____

2. Frank and myself are in charge of the group.   _____

3. Patricia wanted all replies to go to herself.   _____

4. Myself, I prefer chocolate cake.   _____

5. You yourself can make the right choice.   _____

6. Himself is looking for someone to assist him.   _____

7. The teacher gave Daniel and myself some books.   _____

Sometimes, a reflex pronoun is used with its antecedent for emphasis. Which of the above sentences provides an example of this use?

No. _____

Pronoun Cases

1. Subjective case: I, you, he, she, it, we, they, who, whoever
2. Objective case: me, you, him, her, it, us, them, whom, whomever
3. Possessive case: my, mine, your, yours, his, her, hers, its, our, ours, their, theirs, whose

The subjective case is used when the pronoun is the subject of a sentence.

Examples: **I** went for a walk. **We** went for a walk. **They** went for a walk. **You** went for a walk.

The objective case is used when the pronoun is a part of the predicate and specifically the object of the verb or of a preposition.

Examples: Julia thanked **him**. Julia thanked **them**. Julia thanked **us**.

Examples: Objects of prepositions (underlined):

John threw the ball <u>to</u> **her**. John smiled <u>at</u> **you**. John walked <u>around</u> **us**.

The possessive case is used to show ownership.

Examples: This is **my** car. That was **our** house. This is **your** hat. That dog is **mine**.

Exercise E

In each of the following sentences, fill in the blanks with the proper pronoun from the choices in parentheses.

1. _____ (whose, who, whoever) books were left on the floor?

2. I looked everywhere for _____ (mine, my, its) house key.

3. _____ (myself, I) will speak first.

4. _____ (whomever, whoever) wins the race will receive a prize.

5. The teacher asked Martin and _____ (I, me) to help arrange the desks.

6. The story interested _____ . (us, we)

7. To _____ (whom, who) are you asking the question?

8. Paul and _____ (I, me) will meet on Saturday.

9. The guest speaker answered questions from _____ (whomever, whoever) asked them.

10. It will be _____ or _____ (them, they / we, us) who will be chosen.

11. Have you lost your eraser? I think this is _____ (hers, yours).

3 Descriptive Words and Phrases

Adjectives and adverbs are descriptive words that add meaning to a sentence by giving the reader additional information.

An adjective describes a noun or a pronoun, often the subject or object of a sentence.

An adverb describes a verb, the action in the sentence. Adverbs often end in "ly" and answer the question "how".

Example: The **tall** boy walked **slowly** down the road.

"Tall" is an adjective describing the noun "boy"; "slowly" is an adverb describing the action of the verb "walked".

Exercise A

Remember: A subject is the doer of the action in the sentence. An object is the receiver of the action in the sentence.

Underline the adjectives and place parentheses ( ) around the adverbs in each sentence below.

There is at least one adjective and one adverb in each sentence.

1. The sly fox slipped quietly through the woods.

2. The black cloud hovered menacingly over the playing field.

3. John, the oldest boy in the class, spoke confidently.

4. The boys often enjoyed playing exciting computer games.

5. The red bicycle suddenly broke down in the middle of the trip.

6. They carefully entered the cold, dark cave.

CHALLENGE

Some words can serve as both adjectives and adverbs. For the sentences below, state whether the underlined words are acting as adjectives or adverbs.

1. The score was a <u>far</u> cry from what we expected. _____

2. He was in great shape and ran <u>far</u>. _____

3. She arrived <u>first</u> because she had a ride. _____

4. This is the <u>first</u> time we have been here. _____

Adverb and Adjective Phrases

A phrase is a group of words that usually begins with a preposition.
Phrases describe nouns, pronouns, and verbs in a sentence. Adverb phrases often answer the questions where, how, or when the action took place.

Example: The girls **in our class** played **on the swings**.

"In our class" explains who the girls are, and is, therefore, an adjective phrase. It is a phrase because it is a group of words beginning with a preposition (in).

"On the swings" explains where the girls were playing. It is a phrase because it, too, begins with a preposition (on).

Exercise B

Underline the adjective phrases and place parentheses ( ) around the adverb phrases in the sentences below.

> Check to see whether the phrase answers the questions "when", "where", and "how". If so, it is likely an adverb phrase.

1. The walk to the store was very difficult during the storm.

2. In the morning, the animals in the barn were fed.

3. The leader of the pack was the large grey wolf.

4. The pens in the desk were the property of the boy in the third row.

5. At the game, we ate our lunch of sandwiches and cookies.

6. During his speech, he dropped the notes of the project.

CHALLENGE

Some words are unnecessary because they are redundant. Cross out the unnecessary adverb in each sentence.

> "Redundant" means that a word or idea is repeated unnecessarily.

1. He was asked to repeat again his question.

2. They should all cooperate together.

3. The students were told to finish up their schoolwork.

4. They returned back from holiday.

5. They divided up the winnings.

A **Preposition** is a connecting word that connects a noun or pronoun to other parts of a sentence.

Prepositions are also used to introduce adjective and adverb phrases.

8 rules for frequently misused prepositions:

1. **at, with** – use "at" with a thing; use "with" when relating to a person.

2. **among, between** – use "among" when referring to more than two; use "between" for two.

3. **beside, besides** – use "beside" to mean next to; use "besides" to mean other than or as well as.

4. **in, into** – use "in" to mean within something or somewhere; use "into" to mean from outside to inside.

5. **differ from, differ in** – use "differ from" to show difference between two people; use "differ in" to state in what the difference lies.

6. **differ about, differ with** – use "differ about" to state a point of difference; use "differ with" to indicate the other person with whom you differ about a certain issue.

7. **enter at, enter into** – use "enter at" for a specific place; use "enter into" to state an arrangement involving others.

8. **live at, live in, live on** – use "live at" to indicate a specific place such as a hotel; use "live in" to indicate a country, province, or town; use "live on" to state a street location or a specific type of location such as a farm.

Exercise C

Select the correct preposition for each sentence below from the choices in parentheses. Refer to the rules above to make your selection.

1. We walked _____ (in, into) the store from the street.

2. Linda, who was taller, _____ (differed with, differed from) her sister.

3. We _____ (entered at, entered into) the front door.

4. My uncle _____ (stays at, stays on) the Imperial Hotel.

5. The teacher divided the tasks _____ (between, among) all the students.

6. My friend was angry _____ (at, with) me.

7. _____ (Besides, Beside) my family, there will be no one else coming for dinner.

8. He _____ (entered at, entered into) an agreement with his parents to clean his room.

9. He rested _____ (besides, beside) the road before continuing his bike ride.

Choose the adverbs and adjectives from the word bank below and write them in the spaces provided to make a more interesting paragraph.

The
School Picnic

generously   challenging   huge
lucky   dark   final   annual   silly
senior   fun   special   ferociously
suddenly   clear   wildly   slowly
quickly   hungry   early   local
gladly   sunny   blue   bright

> Select the most obvious words first. Write your choices in pencil so that you can make changes if necessary. Some words are interchangeable.

Our 1. _____ school picnic was scheduled for the 2. _____ week in June. The 3. _____ students were responsible for organizing the 4. _____ event.

Fortunately, it was a 5. _____ , 6. _____ day. All the students in the school 7. _____ assembled at the 8. _____ park 9. _____ in the morning. The first set of games, which included races, were very 10. _____ . Some of the games such as the egg toss were 11. _____ but 12. _____ . The students 13. _____ participated in hope of winning a special 14. _____ ribbon.

When the games were finished, food was served to the 15. _____ students. The teachers 16. _____ prepared the barbecue to meet the 17. _____ demand for food.

We were very 18. _____ to have such great weather. The sky was 19. _____ all day. 20. _____ , just as we were getting ready to leave, a 21. _____ thunder cloud drifted 22. _____ overhead. In a matter of moments, the rain pelted down 23. _____ . Screaming 24. _____ , we ran for cover.

4 Understanding Verb Forms

Verb–Subject Agreement

A verb is a word that states the action performed by the subject in a sentence. The subject may be a noun, a pronoun, or a clause. Although there are numerous verb forms, verbs must agree in person and number with their subjects.

Exercise A

In each sentence below, place the correct verb that agrees in person and number with the subject of the sentence.

Verb–Subject
Agreement

1. She _____ (makes, make) her bed each morning before school.

2. The automobile _____ (need, needed) many repairs.

3. We _____ (wished, wishes) for good weather during our vacation.

4. The boys _____ (plays, play) football in the park.

5. The friend of the girls _____ (arrive, arrived) here yesterday.

6. Where _____ (is, are) the other twin brother?

7. The six fish _____ (cost, costs) more than twenty dollars.

Compound Subjects

If the compound subject has two different nouns joined by "and", then it should be treated as a plural subject; but, if the compound subject represents two items that go together to make a single unit, then it is treated as a singular subject.

Exercise B

Singular subjects connected by "or" or "nor" take a singular verb.

1. Neither Sharon nor Victoria _____ (is, are) going to see the movie.

2. Singing and dancing _____ (requires, require) a lot of energy.

3. Tea and toast _____ (are, is) a simple refreshment.

4. He and I _____ (is, are) playing on the same team.

5. Apple pie and ice cream _____ (is, are) one of her favourite treats.

6. Philip or Craig _____ (play, plays) the piano.

When a compound subject is made up of both a singular and a plural noun separated by "either – or" or "neither – nor", place the plural noun second and make the verb agree.

7. Either John or his friends _____ (has, have) the proper address for the party.

8. Neither her mother nor her sisters _____ (realize, realizes) what time it is.

Fractions and Nouns of Quantity

With fractions, the verb agrees with the noun (object of the preposition) in the phrase. If measures of quantity, distance, time, and amount are meant to be single units, use a singular verb.

Exercise C

1. One quarter of the students _____ (was, were) late for school.

2. Half of the highway _____ (were, was) closed for repair.

3. Thirty dollars _____ (have, has) been put aside for the cost of the food.

4. 18 years _____ (are, is) a long time to be in school.

5. Two years _____ (have, has) gone by since the last time I met her.

6. 30% of the people living in the town _____ (is, are) over sixty.

Indefinite Pronoun Agreement

Because indefinite pronouns do not refer to specific things, it can be difficult to decide whether they require a singular or plural verb.

Examples: anyone, everyone, no one, somebody (singular)

both, few, many, several (plural)

all, any, most, more, none, some, enough (singular or plural, depending on the noun they refer to)

Exercise D

1. Many _____ (are, is) called, but few _____ (is, are) chosen.

2. All of the food _____ (were, was) eaten.

3. Nobody _____ (wants, want) to be the first to speak out.

4. None of the boys _____ (wants, want) to be the captain of the team.

5. Everyone _____ (agree, agrees) to help clean up the mess.

6. Somebody _____ (has, have) told her the secret.

Active and Passive Verb Voice

The voice of a verb indicates whether the subject of the verb is the performer of the action of the verb, or whether the subject is the receiver of the action of the verb.

Examples: John threw the ball through the window.
The subject "John" is doing the throwing.

The ball was thrown through the window by John.
The subject "ball" is receiving the action.

Exercise E

Write "Active" or "Passive" after each sentence below.

1. The students enjoyed doing science experiments.   _____

2. The game was played during the lunch hour.   _____

3. She called her friend on the telephone.   _____

4. The teacher is being asked to teach at another school.   _____

5. A party is being organized by the students.   _____

A **Transitive Verb** directs action towards a noun or pronoun. This noun or pronoun that is the receiver of the action of the verb is called an object.

Example: Jake (subject) dropped (verb) the book (object) on the floor.
"The book" is the receiver of the action of the verb.

Exercise F

Underline the transitive verbs in the following sentences and place parentheses ( ) around the objects of the verbs in the sentences.

Remember: The direct object answers the question "what" or "whom".

1. They finished their homework before going out to play.

2. He sailed his boat across the lake.

3. Whenever it is cold outside, she wears a heavy sweater.

4. If we don't play well, we will lose the game.

5. Are you eating your dinner now?

6. He ate meat and potatoes for supper.

An **Intransitive Verb** indicates an action not directed towards an object. An intransitive verb does not have an object. A verb is also intransitive if the intended or implied object is left out.

Examples: The children played happily in the park.
The teacher asked.

Exercise G

Indicate whether the verbs in the sentences below are transitive or intransitive by placing "TR" or "INT" in the spaces provided. Underline the verbs.

In the first sentence on the left, there is no object receiving the action of the verb "played". In the second example, the object is implied but not stated.

1. We watched the baseball game from across the street. _____

2. The ball was thrown from the pitcher to the catcher. _____

3. The volleyball team won the tournament championship. _____

4. The fans watched intensely as the home team lost the game. _____ _____

5. When the relatives arrived, they unpacked their bags. _____ _____

6. The girls sang in the school choir and the spectators were delighted by the music. _____ _____

7. The students, with the help of their teacher, were successful in school. _____

CHALLENGE

Change the verb voice in each sentence below.

1. The children gathered flowers from the garden.

   _____

2. She met her friends at the bus stop.

   _____

3. The dog ate the scraps on the table.

   _____

4. The children were entertained by the clown.

   _____

If the voice is active, change it to passive; if the voice is passive, change it to the active voice.

5 Verb Tenses

The Present Tense

Simple Present and Progressive Present
The simple present includes events that are happening at the time of speaking as well as events that go on all the time.

Simple: He **lives** in Toronto.
Progressive: He **is living** in Toronto.

Present Perfect Progressive
This verb tense indicates action that is going on at present but started in the past.

Example: He **has been living** in Toronto.
              Note: The present perfect tense uses auxiliary (helper) words "has been".

Exercise A

Change the verb in each sentence to the tense required in parentheses.

1. Paula walks to school instead of taking the bus. (Progressive present)

   _____

2. I had a new bicycle. (Simple present)

   _____

3. She is walking her dog in the park. (Present perfect progressive)

   _____

4. We were swimming in the lake. (Present perfect progressive)

   _____

5. My friends and I planned to have a party. (Progressive present)

   _____

6. My dog will chase the ball. (Present perfect progressive)

   _____

The Past Tense

Simple Past

The simple past refers to events that took place in the past. These events have been completed and do not extend to the present.

Example: The team **won** the final game.

Past Progressive

This tense indicates actions that were continuing or actions that occurred in the past but with limitations.

Example: The team **was winning** the game the last time we checked the score.

Past Perfect

This tense indicates past action that was completed by a certain time in the past or before another past action occurred.

Example: The team **had won** the game by the time we checked the score.

Past Perfect Progressive

This tense indicates continuing action in the past that began before a certain time, or before another action in the past occurred.

Example: The team **had been winning** the game until the other team scored a goal.

Exercise B

In each of the following sentences, change the verb in parentheses to the tense indicated.

1. Children _____ (play) on the swings there. (Past progressive)

2. The sun _____ (shine) on the flowers. (Simple past)

3. The news _____ (arrive) by Internet transmission. (Past perfect progressive)

4. Many people _____ (watch) the World Cup. (Past perfect)

5. His cousin _____ (visit) them in January. (Past perfect progressive)

6. He _____ (help) his father cut the grass. (Simple past)

7. The students _____ (do) their homework together. (Past perfect)

8. The phone rang when we _____ (have) dinner. (Past progressive)

9. No one _____ (try) that before. (Past perfect)

The Future Tense
Simple Future
This tense indicates action that will occur in the future.
Example: They **will work** hard in school.

Future Progressive
This tense indicates continuing action in the future.
Example: They **will be working** hard in school.

Future Perfect
This tense indicates action that will be completed in the future before a certain time or before a certain event.
Example: They **will have worked** hard in school before the end of the year arrives.

Future Perfect Progressive
This tense indicates continuing action that will be completed by a certain time in the future.
Example: They **will have been working** hard in school by the time school ends.

Exercise C

In each of the following sentences, change the verb in parentheses to the tense indicated.

1. We _____ (wait) for the train to enter the terminal. (Simple future)

2. The game _____ (is played) in bad weather. (Future perfect progressive)

3. Sophia _____ (give) a lot of her time to help the school. (Future perfect)

4. I _____ (go) to see my grandfather play in a bowling tournament. (Simple future)

5. Many people _____ (want) to listen to the politician speak. (Future perfect)

6. We _____ (watch out) for our friends who are arriving any time now. (Simple future)

7. Our teacher _____ (congratulate) us on our success. (Future perfect progressive)

8. The distance runner _____ (pace) himself during the race. (Future perfect)

Complete the following sentences in your own way using the appropriate verb tenses.

1. When he saw me, _____

2. Fred usually walks to school, but yesterday _____

3. For the past month, our teacher _____

4. If you happen to see Jason, please _____

5. Next week, all of us _____

6. By the time the rain stopped, _____

7. Do you know where my folder is? I _____

8. The door closed just as we _____

CHALLENGE

Dad and I <u>went</u> to a ball game last weekend. We <u>were</u> late because of the traffic. By the time we <u>reached</u> the stadium, the rival team <u>had scored</u> twice. How disappointing! Next time, we <u>will make</u> sure to allow more time for traffic.

Write a short paragraph making use of three of the tenses you have learnt.

_____

_____

_____

_____

_____

_____

6 The Sentence and Its Parts

Subject and Predicate

A sentence is made up of words that express a complete thought. Basically, a sentence is divided into two parts: the subject and the predicate.

The subject contains a noun or pronoun that usually performs the action of the verb in the sentence.

Included in the subject of a sentence are the modifiers of the subject – descriptive words such as adjectives and adjective phrases.

The predicate of a sentence contains the verb (action word) and its modifiers – descriptive words such as adverbs and adverb phrases.

Exercise A

Draw a line to separate the subject and the predicate in each sentence below. Place parentheses ( ) around the modifiers of both the subject and the verb. Include adjective and adverb phrases with your modifiers.

1. The (old) man | walked (slowly) (down the street).

2. The cute kitten was playing with a ball of wool.

3. The old building was being demolished by the wrecking crew.

4. The uncertain weather caused a delay in our plans.

5. Water-skiing is difficult if you are a beginner.

6. We walked two miles to get to town.

7. The hot sun shines brightly in the sky.

8. I was laughing at the clown.

Articles are classified as adjectives but they do not describe a noun in the same detailed way that an adjective would. "A", "an", and "the" are articles also known as noun determiners. They help us distinguish which nouns are being referred to in a sentence. There are two types of articles: "definite" and "indefinite".

Example: He took **the** ball from **a** cupboard.

"The" is a definite article because it tells exactly which ball was taken. "A" describes "cupboard" but it is an indefinite article because it doesn't state which cupboard is being referred to.

> Use "a" before a noun beginning with a consonant, "an" before a noun beginning with a vowel, and "the" to indicate a specific noun.

Exercise B

Place the proper article before the noun in each of the following sentences.

1. _____ (a, an) apple a day keeps the doctor away.

2. He placed _____ (the , a) books that he had finished reading on his shelf.

3. Which of _____ (an, a, the) players will score the winning goal?

4. Paul is _____ (an, a) enthusiastic student.

5. Sophia felt _____ (the, a) sudden urge to eat chocolate.

6. This is _____ (a, an, the) great day to get outdoors.

Direct and Indirect Objects
A direct object is the receiver of the action of a transitive verb.
An indirect object is a noun or pronoun that tells to whom or for whom the action of the verb is directed.

Example: John gave Susan his book.
"John" is the subject of the sentence and the performer of the action.
The verb "gave" represents the action (transitive) in the sentence.
The "book" is the direct object that receives the action of the verb "gave".
"Susan" is the indirect object because the action of the verb is directed to her.

Exercise C

Underline the direct objects and place parentheses ( ) around the indirect objects in the sentences below.

1. Paula bought her lunch at the restaurant.

2. The teacher gave the students an assignment.

3. His coach gave him a warm welcome when he came off the ice.

4. The parents gave their children treats for lunch.

5. She told her friend the truth about what happened.

6. Jeremy took all his gym equipment home to be washed.

7. The driver told the passengers the good news.

8. The clerk sold us a ticket to the concert.

9. Our teacher prepared us for an important literacy test.

Object of a Preposition

The noun following a preposition in a phrase is an object of the preposition.

Example: The student sat **in** his **desk**.

The phrase "in his desk" is introduced by the preposition "in". The noun "desk" is the object of the preposition "in".

There are 10 objects of prepositions below; one sentence has 3 objects!

Underline the objects of the prepositions in the following sentences.

1. In the morning, we prepared to leave for school.

2. Into the cool water dove the overheated children.

3. We rowed our boat far from the shore.

4. The students in our class prepared to face the chilly weather at recess.

5. Over the hill and beyond the horizon, the sun set in the ocean.

6. The cat ventured into the night under the moonlight.

Other Predicate Complements

A **Predicate Nominative** is a noun or noun substitute that follows an intransitive verb and refers to the subject.

Example: The winner was **Paul**.

A **Predicate Adjective** is an adjective that follows an intransitive verb and describes the subject.

Example: Paul is **tall**.

Identify each italicized word in the following sentences by placing "A" for predicate nominative or "B" for predicate adjective in the space provided.

1. Although she didn't succeed, this student is still very *clever*.   _____

2. Paul is the *creator* of the new game that we all play at recess time.   _____

3. She was *wise* because she prepared herself for whatever might happen.   _____

4. Richard was the *leader* ; Brian was the *follower*.   _____ _____

5. The dessert was *delicious* but it was also *fattening*. _____ _____

6. Whenever we see her, she is always *happy*. _____

CHALLENGE

Indentify the parts of speech in each sentence. Choose from the parts of speech listed below for your answers. Write the letters in the parentheses.

The adverb and adjective phrases are underlined. Identify the type of phrase for each.

A. article   **B.** noun   **C.** adjective   **D.** adjective phrase
E. verb   **F.** adverb   **G.** direct object
H. object of preposition   **I.** preposition   **J.** adverb phrase

1. The losing team shook hands <u>with the winners</u>.
   (   )(   ) (   ) (   ) (   ) (   )

2. The students <u>of Maple Avenue school</u> collected money
   (   )(   ) (   ) (   ) (   )

   <u>for a charity</u>.
   (   )

3. An old friend <u>of mine</u> came <u>to my school</u> today <u>before noon</u>.
   ( )( )(   )(   )(   ) (   )(   ) (   )

4. The man told me to go <u>over the hill</u> <u>to the little farm house</u>.
   ( )( )( )( )(   )(   )(   )

5. The boy <u>in blue jeans</u> is the cousin <u>of my friend</u>.
   ( )( )(   )( )( )(   )(   )

6. Many students <u>of grade 3</u> are waiting excitedly <u>for the play</u> to start.
   (   )(   )(   )(   )(   ) (   )( )( )

7. Christa is leaving Canada <u>for Japan</u> tonight.
   (   ) (   ) (   )(   )(   )

7 Compound and Complex Sentences

Definitions

A **Simple Sentence** is made up of one subject and one verb.

A **Compound Sentence** is made up of two or more simple sentences joined by a conjunction (and, if, but, or, so...) or by a semi-colon (;).

Exercise A

Complete the compound sentences with the simple sentences in the box. Use the correct conjunctions.

Use each conjunction only once.

because   if

and   so

• I study very hard for the test.
• We could go out and play.
• I saw a squirrel climb a tree.
• We all played games.

1. I walked in the park _____

2. We did all our homework _____

3. Her birthday party was a lot of fun _____

4. I will receive a high mark in Science _____

The Subordinate Clause

A sentence is sometimes called an "independent clause" because a sentence is a complete thought and can stand on its own without needing more information to complete its meaning.

A subordinate clause is a "dependent clause" because it needs an independent clause to complete its meaning.

Like an independent clause (sentence), a subordinate clause has a noun and a verb. It has a connecting word or conjunction usually at the beginning.

Examples: 1. although I enjoy eating pizza
2. when I was walking home from school
3. after we watched the game on television

Did you notice that all of the clauses in the examples have nouns and verbs but are incomplete sentences because they do not give enough information?

Exercise B

After each sentence or clause below, state whether it is an independent clause (complete sentence) or a dependent clause (incomplete sentence) by placing "IC" for an independent clause or "DC" for a dependent clause in the space provided.

1. Winter is my favourite season of the year. _____

2. When summer arrives. _____

3. After the boys played baseball and put away the equipment. _____

4. Because it was a beautiful sunny day. _____

5. When are you leaving? _____

6. Look out, the shelf is falling! _____

7. Where does the new student live? _____

8. If you choose to play instead of work. _____

9. The girls beat the boys in the spelling contest. _____

10. When I get home from school. _____

11. Before he could have the chance to read the answers. _____

12. Give it to Daniel. _____

13. Unless you let me go with you. _____

14. He rode his bicycle to school every day. _____

Clauses and Phrases

There is difference between clauses and phrases.

A **phrase** is a group of words that does not have both a noun and a verb, and begins with a preposition (in, under, of...). A phrase describes either a noun or a verb.

Examples: in the box, under the table, behind the bookshelf, of the class, at the game...

A **clause** contains a noun and a verb, and begins with a subordinating conjunction (whenever, after, because...).

Exercise C

Identify each of the following groups of words as either a phrase or a subordinate clause. Write "phrase" or "clause" in the space provided. If you find a complete sentence, write the word "sentence".

> There are three complete sentences. Did you find them?

1. Whenever I ask a question.   _____
2. Towards the street corner.   _____
3. They walked under the bridge.   _____
4. If it rains this afternoon.   _____
5. They play golf on Saturdays.   _____
6. Nothing is better than a hot slice of pizza.   _____
7. Below the window ledge.   _____
8. Because they asked me to help them.   _____

Adverbial and Adjectival Clauses

An **adverbial** clause does the same job as an adverb – it tells where or when the action of the verb takes place.

Example: We did not leave **until everyone boarded the bus**.
The clause "until everyone boarded the bus" tells when the action took place.

An **adjectival** clause does the work of an adjective – it gives information about a noun in the sentence.

Example: My friend Randall, **who lives in London, England**, sends me e-mail messages once a week.
The clause "who lives in London, England" describes Randall.

Exercise D

Indicate by writing ADV (adverbial) or ADJ (adjectival) in the space following each sentence the type of clause written in italics.

1. *Whenever they went on holiday*, they always spent too much money.   _____

2. *After we had eaten our lunch*, we played soccer in the park.   _____

3. The teams, *which were chosen by the teacher*, were fair.   _____

4. *If I knew that you were coming over,* I would have stayed home.　　　＿＿＿＿＿＿＿＿＿

5. He was the only one *who knew what we were supposed to do.*　　　＿＿＿＿＿＿＿＿＿

6. I took the bus instead *because I did not have enough money.* ＿＿＿＿＿＿＿＿＿

Exercise E

Add either an independent clause or a dependent clause to each partial sentence below to make a complete sentence.

1. Because the bus was delayed, ＿＿＿＿＿＿＿＿＿＿＿＿＿＿＿＿＿＿＿

2. If you try your best, ＿＿＿＿＿＿＿＿＿＿＿＿＿＿＿＿＿＿＿＿＿＿

3. The restaurant was empty even though ＿＿＿＿＿＿＿＿＿＿＿＿＿＿

＿＿＿＿＿＿＿＿＿＿＿＿＿＿＿＿＿＿＿＿＿＿＿＿＿＿＿＿＿＿＿＿＿

4. While we sat waiting for the movie to begin, ＿＿＿＿＿＿＿＿＿＿

＿＿＿＿＿＿＿＿＿＿＿＿＿＿＿＿＿＿＿＿＿＿＿＿＿＿＿＿＿＿＿＿＿

5. I was frightened on Halloween because ＿＿＿＿＿＿＿＿＿＿＿＿＿

＿＿＿＿＿＿＿＿＿＿＿＿＿＿＿＿＿＿＿＿＿＿＿＿＿＿＿＿＿＿＿＿＿

Exercise F

Write a brief descriptive story on "The Winning Goal" using subordinate clauses in your sentences. Try using these subordinating conjunctions in your sentences.

whenever	because	after	before	while	however

＿＿＿＿＿＿＿＿＿＿＿＿＿＿＿＿＿＿＿＿＿＿＿＿＿＿＿＿＿＿＿＿＿＿＿＿＿

＿＿＿＿＿＿＿＿＿＿＿＿＿＿＿＿＿＿＿＿＿＿＿＿＿＿＿＿＿＿＿＿＿＿＿＿＿

＿＿＿＿＿＿＿＿＿＿＿＿＿＿＿＿＿＿＿＿＿＿＿＿＿＿＿＿＿＿＿＿＿＿＿＿＿

＿＿＿＿＿＿＿＿＿＿＿＿＿＿＿＿＿＿＿＿＿＿＿＿＿＿＿＿＿＿＿＿＿＿＿＿＿

＿＿＿＿＿＿＿＿＿＿＿＿＿＿＿＿＿＿＿＿＿＿＿＿＿＿＿＿＿＿＿＿＿＿＿＿＿

Types of Nouns

 Exercise A

Identify each of the following nouns: simple, proper, compound, and collective.

1. automobile _____
2. doctor _____
3. professor _____
4. fireplace _____
5. mother _____
6. group _____
7. City Hall _____
8. Calgary _____
9. flashlight _____
10. orchestra _____
11. family _____
12. crew _____
13. January _____
14. Doctor Jones _____

Noun Plurals

Exercise B

Write the plural form of the following nouns.

1. boat _____
2. ox _____
3. woman _____
4. coach _____
5. bush _____
6. hero _____
7. wife _____
8. knife _____
9. zoo _____
10. shoe _____
11. cliff _____
12. lady _____

Verbs to Nouns

Exercise C

Change each of the following verbs to its noun form.

1. bakes _____
2. creates _____
3. design _____
4. plays _____
5. thinks _____
6. swim _____
7. teach _____
8. help _____
9. plans _____
10. builds _____
11. speaks _____
12. lie _____

Pronouns

> A pronoun replaces a noun. A noun in a sentence that is replaced by a pronoun is called an antecedent.

Exercise D

For each of the following sentences, choose the correct pronoun to suit the antecedent.

1. The whole group of friends brought _____ (his, her, their) photos.
2. Paul and Peter were early because _____ (he, they, it) left ahead of the others.
3. We brought _____ (our, their) own food for the picnic.
4. My dog loves to play with _____ (its, his, her) rubber bone.
5. We asked _____ (those, them, him) if they would help us.
6. The children played with _____ (their, its, mine) toys by themselves.
7. I was hoping that the teacher would choose _____ (me, I) to be the class representative.

Types of Pronouns

> Do you remember the four types of pronouns: demonstrative, interrogative, relative, and reflexive?

Exercise E

In each of the following sentences, choose the correct pronoun and fill in the blanks. In the space following the sentence, state which type of pronoun it is.

1. _____ (what, which) of the children was crying? _____
2. _____ (who, whose) will be our new teacher? _____
3. Give _____ (those, that, them) pencils to the students. _____
4. He brought a gift _____ (those, that) surprised everyone. _____
5. The person _____ (who, whom) spoke out was embarrassed. _____
6. She wore _____ (herself, themselves) out running too fast. _____

Progress Test 1

Adverbs and Adjectives

Exercise F

Complete the following sentences with suitable adjectives or adverbs.

Adverbs describe verbs; adjectives describe nouns.

> loudly   completely   happily   cleverly   menacingly
> sly   tall   threatening   cheerful   frightened

1. The _____ , little boy called _____ for his mother.
2. The _____ tree shaded the flower garden _____ .
3. The _____ children played _____ in the playground.
4. The _____ , old fox hunted _____ for the unsuspecting mouse.
5. Dark, _____ clouds hovered _____ overhead.

Adjective and Adverb Phrases

Exercise G

Underline the adjective phrases and place parentheses ( ) around the adverb phrases in each sentence below.

Adjective and adverb phrases do the same work in a sentence as adverbs and adjectives.

1. The bird in the bush sang a song of the wild.
2. Under the carpet, he hid his gift of money.
3. In the middle of the night, it began raining.
4. The choir of St. Michael's sang in the church near the village.

Prepositions

Exercise H

Select the proper preposition and fill in the blank in each of the following sentences.

1. She had to decide _____ (among, between) the two choices.
2. He walked _____ (into, in) the house to get out of the cold.
3. My results are different _____ (with, from) the teacher's.
4. The children differed _____ (in, from) the choice of activity.
5. We couldn't agree _____ (to, on) where to go for the game.

Verb-Subject Agreement

Exercise I

Write the correct verb form in the space provided in each of the following sentences.

1. Neither of the girls _____ (wish, wishes) to participate in the choir.

2. Jamie and Andrew _____ (play, plays) on the same hockey team.

3. Peaches and cream _____ (is, are) her favourite dessert.

4. Neither the coach nor the swimmers _____ (wants, want) to practise in the lake.

5. Running and jumping _____ (makes, make) up the hurdle event.

6. Susan or Sharon _____ (choose, chooses) between the participants.

7. One quarter of the students _____ (write, writes) the test in the classroom.

Active and Passive Voice

> With an active voice, the subject performs the action. With the passive voice, the subject is the receiver of the action.

Exercise J

Change the following sentences from active voice to passive, or from passive to active.

1. The car was driven by Patricia's father.

   _____

2. That picture on the wall was drawn by me.

   _____

3. Sam's mother made the birthday cake.

   _____

4. We planted the tree in the backyard.

   _____

5. The alarm was set off by the naughty children.

   _____

Progress Test 1

Transitive and Intransitive Verbs

Transitive verbs direct action towards an object (noun or pronoun) in a sentence. Intransitive verbs do not direct their action to an object.

Exercise K

Identify each of the following sentences as being transitive or intransitive.

1. She invited all her classmates to a barbecue at her home. _____
2. They waited for a long time for the bus. _____
3. Peter phoned his friend after dinner. _____
4. The team was disappointed because they didn't play well. _____
5. Irene made a card for her mother. _____
6. She left without the teacher's permission. _____

Direct and Indirect Objects

A direct object receives the action of the verb. An indirect object tells to whom or to what the action of the verb is directed.

Exercise L

Underline the direct objects and place parentheses ( ) around the indirect objects in each sentence below. Identify the type of object by writing "D" or "I" in the space provided.

Some sentences may have both types of objects. List them in the order they appear.

1. He chased his dog around the yard. _____
2. She gave her the address to her house. _____ _____
3. The rain soaked the flowers in the yard. _____
4. The teacher gave the students homework. _____ _____
5. She called her friend to invite her to go swimming. _____
6. He asked me to go with him. _____
7. His father bought him a new bike. _____ _____

Objects of Prepositions

The noun following a preposition in a phrase is called the object of the preposition.

Exercise M

Underline the objects of the prepositions only. Do not underline direct or indirect objects in the sentences.

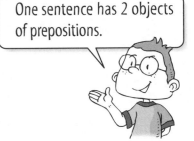

One sentence has 2 objects of prepositions.

1. In the moonlight, we could see quite well.
2. The chair was tucked under the table.
3. After the rainfall, the sun came out.
4. He slept throughout the movie.
5. Over the hill and beyond the farmhouse, we found the lost sheep.

Compound and Complex Sentences

A compound sentence has two simple sentences joined by a conjunction. A complex sentence has a principal clause and a subordinate clause.

Exercise N

Change the simple sentences into compound or complex sentences.

1. The children stopped playing. They were too tired.

   _____

2. I like mangoes. I don't like bananas.

   _____

3. Jason is short. He can play basketball well.

   _____

4. We can go there by subway. We can go there by bus.

   _____

5. I will tell you. You don't tell anyone else.

   _____

8 Verbal, Participle, and Infinitive Phrases

Verbals are verb forms that do not act as verbs in sentences. Instead, they function as nouns, adjectives, and adverbs.

There are three kinds of verbals: participle, gerund, and infinitive.

Participles have been reviewed in a previous unit.

Gerunds are verbals that act as nouns. They look like participles because they end in "ing". Gerunds are often the subject or the object in a sentence.

Example (1): **Skiing** is fun. The word "skiing" is a gerund acting as the subject of the sentence. It is the gerund form of the verb "ski".

Example (2): She enjoys **swimming**. The word "swimming" is a gerund acting as the object of the sentence. It is what is being enjoyed.

Exercise A

Fill in each blank with the gerund form of the verb in parentheses. Circle "Subj." or "Obj." at the end of the sentence to state whether the gerund is the subject or object.

1. _____ (jump) over a puddle can be risky. **Subj.** **Obj.**

2. _____ (fall) from your bicycle can be painful. **Subj.** **Obj.**

3. Paul loves _____ (chew) bubble gum. **Subj.** **Obj.**

4. _____ (win) the game was the only thing that mattered to him.
   Subj. **Obj.**

5. She enjoyed _____ (sip) her tea and _____ (eat) cake.
   Subj. **Obj.**

6. _____ (sing) and _____ (dance) are her favourite activities.
   Subj. **Obj.**

7. Jason is keen on _____ (make) models. **Subj.** **Obj.**

8. Grandpa likes _____ (watch) old movies. **Subj.** **Obj.**

9. _____ (play) street hockey is what they like to do on weekends.
   Subj. **Obj.**

The **Infinitive** is formed by adding the word "to" to a verb. For example, the infinitive form of "run" would be "to run".

Note: "To be" is the infinitive form of the familiar verbs: is, are, was, were.
The infinitive can play the role of a noun, adjective, or an adverb in a sentence.

Example (1): He wanted **to play**.
"To play" is acting as a noun (object). It is what was wanted.

Example (2): There was no time **to work**.
"To work" is acting as an adjective telling what kind of time it is.

Example (3): He was prepared **to clean** the car.
"To clean" is acting as an adverb explaining how he was prepared.

Exercise B

Underline the infinitives in the following sentences and state whether they are acting as nouns, adjectives, or adverbs. Circle your choices.

1. To fly across the sky is thrilling.   **noun**   **adjective**   **adverb**

2. He wanted to speak to his teacher.   **noun**   **adjective**   **adverb**

3. To write a letter is sometimes difficult.   **noun**   **adjective**   **adverb**

4. He was ready to play the hockey game.   **noun**   **adjective**   **adverb**

5. They were happy to come to the party.   **noun**   **adjective**   **adverb**

Present and Past Participles

Participles function as adjectives in a sentence.

Example: The **winning** team received the trophy.
"Winning" is the present participle form of "win" and describes the noun "team".
Therefore it is acting as an adjective.

Exercise C

#3 has two participles.

Underline the participle in each of the following sentences and write the noun that it describes in the space.

1. He woke up the sleeping giant.   _____

2. He swallowed his chewing gum.   _____

3. The swaying branches made rustling noises.   _____

4. The carrying case was handy for travelling.   _____

5. The cutting edge of the knife was very sharp.   _____

A **Participle Phrase** acts as an adjective and begins with a participle.

Example (1): **Standing in the rain**, I got very wet.

"Standing" is the participle, and "Standing in the rain" is the participle phrase. This participle phrase is an adjective phrase describing the pronoun "I".

Example (2): **Thrilled at winning the game**, the players celebrated.

"Thrilled" is the participle, and "Thrilled at winning the game" is the participle phrase. This participle phrase is an adjective phrase describing the noun "players".

Exercise D

Underline the participle phrase in each of the following sentences. Write the noun that it describes in the space following the sentence.

1. Waiting for a long time, the lady read her book. _____

2. The old man climbing the stairs was out of breath. _____

3. Thrilled with the outcome, the winner accepted the praise. _____

4. The students playing in the gym wore running shoes. _____

5. Worried that he would be late for school, the boy ran all the way. _____

6. The orchestra playing a classical tune entertained everyone. _____

7. He followed his friends, hoping not to get lost. _____

8. Delighted with the cake that she baked, the girl gave everyone a piece. _____

9. Frightened by the bulldog, the children ran away from the backyard. _____

10. The woman carrying an umbrella walked slowly in the rain. _____

11. Hearing the bad news, the actress broke into tears. _____

12. The puppy chasing the birds is very cute. _____

13. Surrounded by police, the robber couldn't get away. _____

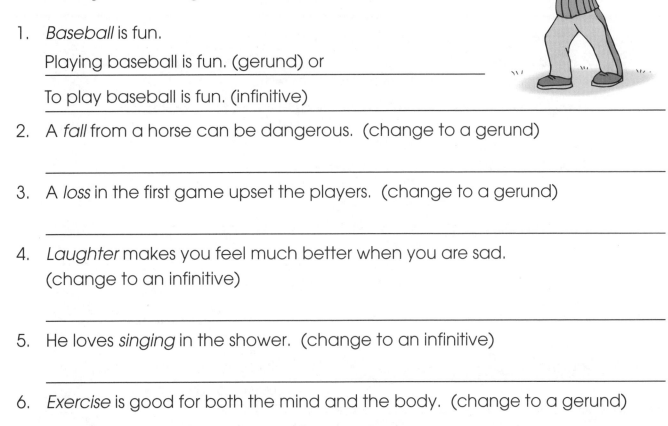

Exercise E

Rewrite each of the sentences below replacing the italicized noun (subject) with a gerund or an infinitive.

1. *Baseball* is fun.

    Playing baseball is fun. (gerund) or

    To play baseball is fun. (infinitive)

2. A *fall* from a horse can be dangerous. (change to a gerund)

    _____

3. A *loss* in the first game upset the players. (change to a gerund)

    _____

4. *Laughter* makes you feel much better when you are sad.
    (change to an infinitive)

    _____

5. He loves *singing* in the shower. (change to an infinitive)

    _____

6. *Exercise* is good for both the mind and the body. (change to a gerund)

    _____

CHALLENGE

Write a paragraph using the participle or infinitive form of the following verbs.

wait	play	excite	hit	shout	surprise

_____

_____

_____

_____

_____

9 Phrases – Noun, Gerund, Appositive, Absolute

A **Noun Phrase** is made up of a noun and all its modifiers. A noun phrase can be a subject, object, or a sentence complement (following the verb to be).

Example (Subject):   **Healthy, green salad** is served in the cafeteria.
The noun phrase "Healthy, green salad" is acting as subject of the verb "is".

Example (Object):   They eat **healthy, green salad**.
The noun phrase "healthy, green salad" is acting as object of the verb "eat".

Example (Complement): A piece of fruit is **a healthy snack**.
The noun phrase "a healthy snack" is the complement to the verb "is".

Exercise A

The noun phrase does not have to be the subject of the sentence.

Match the noun phrases with the sentence remainders by writing letters in the blanks. Then write sentences with them.

Column A

1. fine, colourful silk   _____
2. hot, spicy sauce   _____
3. expensive, costume jewellery   _____
4. scary, ghost stories   _____
5. bright, colourful flags   _____
6. warm, fuzzy blankets   _____

Column B

A. surrounded the Olympic Stadium
B. she wore
C. around the campfire, they told
D. kept us warm all night long.
E. was used to make neckties.
F. was spread on the pizza.

1. _____
2. _____
3. _____
4. _____
5. _____
6. _____

A **Gerund Phrase** is made up of a gerund and its modifiers, objects or complements. A gerund phrase can act as subject of the verb, complement of the verb "to be", direct or indirect object, and object of a preposition.

Rules of Use

A. **Subject**: **Playing football** is a game we all enjoy.

B. **Object**: He likes **playing football** with his friends after school.

C. **Complement**: The greatest excitement is **playing football**.

D. **Object of a Preposition**: He was very good at **throwing a football**. "At" is the preposition; "throwing a football" is object of the preposition.

Exercise B

Underline the gerund phrase in each of the sentences below and write the letter from the rules above that corresponds to the use of the gerund phrase.

1. Laughing out loud disturbed the people in the audience. _____
2. She enjoyed playing the piano in front of a crowd. _____
3. By keeping the news a secret, she gained their trust. _____
4. He practised running around the track. _____
5. Sweeping the floors took a long time. _____
6. Happiness is flying a kite. _____
7. Making muffins is an easy job. _____

Exercise C

Complete the sentences below with a gerund phrase of your own.

1. _____ was a dangerous task.
2. They enjoyed _____ .
3. Danger is _____ .
4. From _____ , they were tired.
5. After _____ , everyone went home.
6. _____ was so much fun.
7. _____ can't solve the problem.
8. I'll never forget _____ .

The Appositive Phrase

A noun phrase that gives another name for the noun or pronoun directly before it in a sentence is called an appositive phrase.

Example: Wayne Gretsky, **a great hockey player**, attended the celebrity banquet.

The phrase "a great hockey player" is the appositive to the proper noun "Wayne Gretsky".

Underline the appositive phrases in the following sentences and add commas where necessary.

1. The cottage we rented the one with the large front porch has a nice beach.

2. That dog the one with the bushy tail belongs to him.

3. He wanted a bicycle one with racing wheels for his birthday.

4. He chose the first seat the one near the window because it had a view.

5. His sister the one in grade three is waiting for him at the front door of the school.

6. He drove the other car the green convertible to work every day.

7. The players those who showed up on time got the most playing time.

8. Snowboarding a sport for the young has become very popular.

9. Health the thing we all desire can be achieved by eating properly.

10. Fatigue the state of exhaustion followed her completion of the marathon.

Form your own appositive phrases. Be sure to include modifying words.

1. The new teacher, _____ , drives a very old car.

2. Chocolate cake, _____ , is delicious with ice cream.

3. We enjoy going to the beach, _____ .

4. He caught the ball, _____ .

5. The highway, _____ , is the route we always take.

6. My neighbour, _____ , borrowed our lawn mower.

7. I like the new boy, _____ .

8. The video game, _____ , is exciting and challenging.

An **Absolute Phrase** is made up of a noun or pronoun and a participle with objects and modifiers. An absolute phrase modifies the entire sentence rather than just a particular word. It may appear anywhere in a sentence and is set off from the sentence by commas.

Examples: The fans cheered the team, **arms waving madly in the air**.
My fear finally controlled, I entered the dentist office.

The boldfaced words above are absolute phrases because they modify the entire sentences.

Exercise F

Underline the absolute phrases in the following sentences and add commas where necessary.

1. The children are fully entertained the clown having made funny balloons for everyone.

2. He ran out of the house his lunch being left behind.

3. He roared down the ice everyone trying to catch him.

4. The ice cream melted chocolate spilling everywhere.

5. The teacher handed out the report cards students waiting anxiously.

6. They lined up for the penalty shot soccer fans standing motionless.

7. People running everywhere the rainstorm unleashed a heavy downpour.

8. Fans lining up for hours the tickets for the rock concert finally went on sale.

Exercise G

Put the absolute phrases with the sentences that they are best suited to modify.

> skiers dotting the hillside   the dog sitting up begging
> the end of the game coming near   the runners taking their marks
> the contestants holding their breath

1. He held up the piece of hamburger, _____ .

2. The starter gun was about to go off, _____ .

3. _____ , the winner was announced.

4. _____ , the racers swerved in and out of the people.

5. _____ , they made one last effort to get the tying goal.

10 Run-On Sentences and Sentence Combining

A **Run-on Sentence** occurs when two sentences are joined together without proper punctuation or connecting words.

Example: I was expecting him earlier he must be delayed.

There are actually two sentences here: "I was expecting him earlier" and "He must be late". This run-on sentence should become two sentences by placing a period after the word "earlier" and placing a capital on the word "he".

In some cases, one part of the run-on sentence can be made into a subordinate clause.

Example: It was raining we used an umbrella.
This run-on sentence can be changed to: Because it was raining, we used an umbrella.

Correct the following run-on sentences by either changing them to two sentences or by making one part a subordinate clause.

1. Lunch was ready we ate in the kitchen.

    _____

2. The door is wide open someone must be home.

    _____

3. He has cut his foot he put a bandage on it.

    _____

4. The buzzer went the game was over.

    _____

5. She read the book it was about a mystery it took place in England.

    _____

6. The train arrived at the station it was half an hour late.

    _____

7. The weather was fine we had a game of baseball.

    _____

8. It was breezy our kites flew high in the sky.

    _____

Sentence Combining

The following short sentences can be combined to make longer sentences.

Exercise B

Remember to use conjunctions and subordinating conjunctions to create longer, more detailed sentences.

Combine each group of sentences into one sentence.

1. The cat mewed. The cat was hungry. The cat wanted milk.

   _____

2. The car was new. The car was shiny. The car was red.

   _____

3. He was a student. His school was St. Patrick's. He was in grade four.

   _____

4. She wore a coat. The coat was yellow. The coat was a ski jacket.

   _____

5. You should answer questions. You should raise your hand.

   _____

6. There was homework. The homework was mathematics. The homework was plenty.

   _____

7. The game was delayed. The game was baseball. The delay was because of rain.

   _____

8. The children participated in a race. The race was 100 metres. The race was in the schoolyard.

   _____

Exercise C

Join the most obvious ones first.

Choose a sentence from Column A that could be combined with a sentence from Column B. Write each new sentence in the space provided.

Column A

1. The mouse was frightened.
2. The snow was like powder.
3. The bird built a nest.
4. He couldn't find his key.
5. The little girl was crying.
6. They sailed on an ocean liner.
7. They went to the baseball game.
8. The dresser drawers were full.
9. The players drank water.
10. The morning dew melted.

Column B

- She thought that she was lost.
- He was locked out of the house.
- They ate peanuts and cracker jacks.
- The cat was ready to pounce.
- There was a break in the game.
- The skiing was excellent.
- The sun came up.
- It used twigs and bits of straw.
- They had a wonderful vacation.
- There was not enough room for his clothes.

1. _____
2. _____
3. _____
4. _____
5. _____
6. _____
7. _____
8. _____
9. _____
10. _____

Exercise D

Below is a passage containing short, choppy sentences. Combine the sentences that are common in topic. Rewrite the new paragraph in the space below.

Before you start combining the sentences, draw a line separating the sentences into groups that have common topics. Add words as needed. Change some phrases to adjectives. Avoid repeating words.

The Air Canada Centre is a large sports facility. The Air Canada Centre is in Toronto. The Air Canada Centre is downtown. Building of the centre started in 1997. Building of the centre was finished in 1999. The Air Canada Centre is home to the Toronto Maple Leafs. The Air Canada Centre is home to the Toronto Raptors. The first game played there was hockey. The first game was between the Toronto Maple Leafs and the Montreal Canadiens. The first hockey game was on February 20, 1999. The first Raptor game played in the Air Canada Centre was on February 21, 1999. The first Raptor game played there was against the Vancouver Grizzlies. Often there are special events going on there. There are meetings there. There are concerts there. There are community events there. The Air Canada Centre has seats. It has 19,800 seats for basketball games. It has 18,800 seats for hockey games.

The Air Canada Centre

_____

_____

_____

_____

_____

_____

_____

_____

_____

_____

_____

11 Punctuation (1)

Exercise A

Punctuate each of the following sentences. Write the type of sentence in the space provided.

1. Look out   _____

2. What time is it   _____

3. It was an unusually hot day   _____

4. What a hot day   _____

5. Never do that again   _____

6. Do as you are told   _____

7. Help   _____

8. It was nice of him to offer his help
    even though he was busy   _____

9. Do you know which team got the
    champion in yesterday's match   _____

An **Apostrophe** (**'**) is used to show possession of a noun. It is also used to indicate that one or more letters are missing from a word or that one or more numbers are missing from a number.

Example (1): missing number – He played in the '99 Stanley Cup finals.
             The apostrophe replaces the numbers "19" in 1999.

Example (2): contraction – We didn't stop for lunch today.
             The apostrophe replaces the letter "o" in the word "not".

Example (3): possession – This book is Susie's.
             The apostrophe before the "s" shows possession.

Note: It is easy to confuse "its" and "it's".

"Its" is the possessive form of "it".

"It's" is the contracted form of "it is".

Exercise B

Complete the Contraction Chart. Fill in either the contraction or the expanded form of each word in the blank space.

	Expanded	Contracted
1.	could not	
2.	would not	
3.		I'd
4.	do not	
5.	cannot	
6.		you'll
7.	does not	
8.		he'd
9.	he has	
10.	should not	
11.		let's
12.	will not	
13.	is not	
14.		I've
15.	must not	

Possessives

1. Add an "s" to a singular noun to form the possessive case.
   Example: This was the cat**'s** collar.

2. If a plural noun does not end in "s", add "'s" to form the possessive case.
   Example: The children**'s** playground is behind the building.

3. Add only an apostrophe to plural nouns that end in "s".
   Example: The clowns**'** costumes were very colourful.

4. To singular nouns that end in "s", add "'s".
   Example: Dickens**'s** novels were written many years ago.
   Although "Dickens" ends in an "s", it is a singular proper noun.

Note: Possessive pronouns do not require possessive endings.

Make each word below possessive and rewrite it in the space provided. Write the rule # in the parentheses following each word.

1. people _____ ( ) 2. person _____ ( )

3. women _____ ( ) 4. boys _____ ( )

5. players _____ ( ) 6. boy _____ ( )

7. hers _____ ( ) 8. class _____ ( )

9. Keats _____ ( ) 10. geese _____ ( )

11. children _____ ( ) 12. Dennis _____ ( )

13. babies _____ ( ) 14. cat _____ ( )

CHALLENGE

Each sentence below has missing apostrophes. Place a line through each word missing the apostrophe. Make the correction directly above it.

The number in parentheses at the end of each sentence tells you how many apostrophes are missing in each sentence.

1. Pauls coat wasnt left in the cloakroom. (2)

2. Its two oclock but it isnt too late to go out and play. (3)

3. I cant find my picture showing my championship team of 98. (2)

4. The bike was Susans but it wasnt the right size for her. (2)

5. Be very quiet and shell never know we were here. (1)

6. Lets not play tricks on him because it isnt nice. (2)

7. We woke Pauls dog because its time for its walk. (2)

8. Id have waited for you but you took too long. (1)

9. Dont forget to bring Louiss book with you. (2)

10. Whats the matter with your dog? (1)

Colons

1. Use a colon to introduce a list of items.

   Example: The following are John's favourite sports: baseball, basketball, tennis, and golf.

2. Use a colon to separate hours from minutes when using numbers to state time.

   Examples: 4:30 p.m.   11:01 a.m.

3. Use a colon to separate long quotations.

4. Use a colon to introduce an explanation.

   Example: Hockey equipment is necessary: a helmet, a face mask, chin pads, and shoulder pads.

Exercise D

Insert a colon where necessary in the following passage.

The Camping Trip

There are six colons missing.

The day arrived for our camping trip. We packed the following items a tent, a flashlight, a sleeping bag, and a cooler. Our guide gave us this important advice do not leave food around the tent after dark. He also explained "It is important to respect nature and the animals of the woodlands. Remember, you are visiting their territory. Treat it as if it was your own." We left home at 630 a.m. and arrived at the campsite at 1100. It took nearly two hours to set up camp because we had to take care of the following duties clearing the site, hammering in the tent pegs, fetching water, and setting up a campfire.

12 Punctuation (2)

The Comma – Rules of Use

1. Commas are used to separate three or more items in a list.

   Example: At the zoo they saw lions, tigers, elephants, and giraffes.

2. Commas are used to separate phrases and clauses in a series.

   Example: He promised to come home after school, cut the grass, and clean out the garage.

   The above example shows that clauses need to be separated when they are presented as a list of things to do.

3. Commas are used to set off the person you are talking to.

   Example: John, hand me that wrench.

4. Commas are used to separate the name of a city and a province, and between the day and the year of a date.

   Example: They moved to Toronto, Ontario on July 12, 2001.

Add commas where necessary. Place the rule number for the comma use in each sentence in the space provided.

> The number in parentheses at the end of the sentence tells you how many commas are needed in each sentence.

1. She wanted to finish school to go to college and to get a good job. (2) _____

2. We worked ate slept and awoke the next day before they arrived. (3) _____

3. We visited our relatives in Saskatoon Alberta. (1) _____

4. His birthday was August 14 1992. (1) _____

5 We ate soup sandwiches cake and ice cream for lunch. (3) _____

6. Dad will you drive me to my friend's house? (1) _____

7. Playing hockey going skiing and snowboarding are my favourite things to do. (2) _____

8. The Raptors the Leafs and the Argos all play in Toronto Ontario. (3) _____

Direct quotations are set off from the rest of the sentences by a comma following the last word before the quotation. If the quotation comes first, the comma is placed after the last word of the quotation.

Examples: His friend said, "Can you come to the movies with me?"
"I'm going to a movie," his friend said.

Note: If the quotation is followed by a question mark or an exclamation mark, no comma will follow.

Examples: "Where are you going?" he asked.
"Leave me alone!" he screamed.

Exercise B

Place a comma where necessary in the following sentences.

There are only 6 commas needed in the sentences below.

1. "What do you want to eat for supper?" his mother asked.

2. "I wish we had school during the summer" said Susan.

3. "Don't touch that wire!" screamed the electrician.

4. "Do you have any apples pears or oranges?" asked the lady.

5. "Be careful!" he shouted. "There are snakes spiders and rats in the pit."

6. "We have to go now" Danny said.

Commas and Subordinate (Dependent) Clauses

Remember, a dependent clause is a group of words that has a noun and a verb, but depends on an independent clause to complete its meaning. A comma separates the dependent clause from the independent clause when the dependent clause appears first in a sentence.

Exercise C

Underline the dependent clause and add a comma if one is needed.

1. While he was walking home he saw a dog chase a cat.

2. Susan and Julie were excited while they cheered at the hockey game.

3. After they watched the movie they bought ice cream.

4. Whenever he runs in cold weather he gets a sore throat.

5. Because they were late they didn't get any food.

6. If it rains tomorrow we'll have to cancel the trip.

Commas are also used to introduce and to close a friendly letter. Examples: "Dear Mrs. Johnson," or "Sincerely yours," or "Yours truly,".

CHALLENGE

In the following passage, there are commas necessary for a variety of reasons as stated in the rules. Read the passage carefully and insert commas where necessary.

There are 17 commas needed.

The Wax Museum

"Is everyone ready?" asked Miss Jackson. She then announced "The bus is waiting outside." The students put on their coats picked up their knapsacks pulled out their bus tickets and formed a line. Whenever the students took a class trip they were very excited. Today they were going to visit the wax museum located in Niagara Falls Ontario. The museum was very interesting because it had numerous famous people displayed in wax form. John Lennon Elvis Presley John F. Kennedy and Pierre Elliot Trudeau

were a few of the famous people on display. Because the wax figures were so lifelike it was a very spooky experience. One of the students screamed "That wax figure moved!" We all heard this and ran outside. Because we had now left the museum the teacher suggested that we eat lunch. After lunch we walked to the park looked at the Falls and returned to the bus. Although our trip was shortened by the scary incident we had a good time.

The **Semicolon** takes the place of a conjunction. It joins two independent clauses. It is best to use a semicolon with clauses that are closely related in meaning. Semicolons are also used when one independent clause completes or adds to the information of another independent clause.

Using a semicolon will help you avoid writing a run-on sentence.

Example: I enjoy playing sports; however, I have injured my knee.

Exercise D

Join the pairs of clauses to form sentences using semicolons.

Notice that each independent clause has a subject and a verb; therefore, each independent clause is a proper sentence. Choose independent clauses that are either common in subject or add more information to the first independent clause.

Column A

1. I bought her a birthday gift
2. Hockey is my favourite sport
3. She was the smartest girl in the class
4. The teacher arrived late today
5. Never before have we had such weather
6. It was a great celebration
7. The students assembled in the gymnasium
8. The buses were running late
9. My dog loves to run
10. Look up to the sky
11. The dentist gave him a needle

Column B

- her car broke down
- you can see the Milky Way
- the principal was going to speak to them
- his face went numb
- I love to stick-handle the puck
- he really likes to fetch a ball
- she always got the highest marks
- it was something she needed
- the winds howled all night long
- we all ate cake and ice cream
- instead, we took the subway

1. _____

2. _____

3. _____

4. _____

5. _____

6. _____

7. _____

8. _____

9. _____

10. _____

11. _____

13 Capitalization, Abbreviation, and Quotation Marks

Capital Letters must be used in the following cases:

1. To begin a sentence: **H**e played the piano.

2. With proper names such as people, places, cities, towns, countries: **J**ohn **S**mith, **T**oronto, **N**ew **Y**ork **Y**ankees, **P**earson **A**irport

3. For book, song, movie, and TV show titles: **R**omeo and **J**uliet, **J**ingle **B**ells, **CFTO N**ews, **T**he **W**izard of **O**z

4. For days of the week, months of the year: **T**uesday, **O**ctober 3

5. Place capitals on short forms such as **M**r., **M**iss, **M**rs., **D**r., and **S**t.

6. Place capitals on the names of holidays such as **C**hristmas, **T**hanksgiving, and **E**aster.

Place capital letters where necessary in each of the following sentences. Place capitals over the small case words that you are correcting.

> The number in parentheses tells you how many capital letters are needed in each sentence.

1. mr. and mrs. smith arrived in toronto on the third of november. (5)

2. he read "the hobbit" by j.r.r. tolkien. (7)

3. "harry potter" books are very popular. (2)

4. she visited her doctor, dr. johnson, whose office was on main st. (5)

5. at christmas, the children sang "jingle bells". (4)

6. we went to the skyDome to see the blue jays play against the minnesota twins. (6)

7. he watched a show entitled "animals of africa" on discovery channel. (5)

8. on monday, we have english class and on wednesday, we have french class. (5)

9. elton john recorded "goodbye england's rose" as a tribute to princess diana. (7)

10. we watched a disney film entitled "beauty and the beast". (4)

11. mr. todd dixon, our teacher, brought his dog, spot, to school. (4)

12. our computer runs on "windows me" with microsoft word. (6)

Tricky Capitalization

1. When the kinship name of a relative precedes the proper name of the relative, both names are capitalized.

   Example: **A**unt **J**oan and **U**ncle **B**ill came for dinner.

   but not – I went to my aunt's house for dinner.

2. Government offices require capitalization: **M**inistry of **L**abour, **D**epartment of **T**ransportation, **F**ederal **B**ureau of **I**nvestigation, **C**entral **I**ntelligence **A**gency.

3. Capitalize compass points when they refer to a precise location.

   Example: He went out **W**est to find a job. He was originally from the **E**ast.

   but not – He moved to the east end of town. He visited western Europe.

4. Capitalize adjective forms of proper names such as **I**talian, **G**erman, **B**ritish, **F**rench, the **S**mith family, **P**anama **C**anal, **Y**onge **S**treet.

5. Capitalize the name of a professional title when it describes a proper noun: **D**octor **S**mith, **P**rofessor **W**illiams, **S**enator **W**right, **P**resident **B**ush, **P**rime **M**inister **J**ean **C**hretien.

Exercise B

Place capital letters where necessary in each of the following sentences. Place capitals over the small case words that you are correcting.

1. He worked for the ministry of the environment.

2. doctor richards had his office in the cn tower.

3. We boarded a plane for our trip to eastern europe.

4. He lived in the east end of toronto.

5. My aunt hilda's moved out west; I will visit her next fall.

6. uncle adam worked for parks and recreation for the town of ajax.

7. My teacher was known as professor sanderson when he taught at oxford university.

8. When we were in eastern Europe, we travelled to italy and enjoyed italian food.

9. My uncle, professor jones, sent a letter to the premier of Ontario, mike harris.

10. the chunnel connects britain and france.

11. Which planet is bigger, venus or mars?

12. I went to metro zoo with uncle tommy yesterday.

Common Abbreviations

The following is a list of common abbreviations that you should know:

apt. – apartment	Dr. – Drive	Pres. – President
assoc. – association	etc. – et cetera	Prof. – Professor
Ave. – avenue	ft. – foot	Rd. – Road
Blvd. – boulevard	Gov. – Governor	Sgt. – Sergeant
Capt. – Captain	Jr. – Junior	Sr. – Senior / Sister
Co. – Company	Ltd. – limited	St. – Saint / Street
cont. – continued	Mt. – Mount / Mountain	supt. – superintendent
Dr. – Doctor	No. – number	vs. – versus / against

Exercise C

Test yourself with abbreviations that are common to you. Circle the proper abbreviation for each of the following words.

1. centimetres	cnt. cm. cent.	2. ounces	ozs. ounc. oz.
3. millimetres	mill. mm. Mil.	4. quarts	qt. qts. qua.
5. pounds	pou. llb. lb.	6. feet	ft. fe. fee.
7. inches	inch. inc. in.	8. miles	mls. mil. mi.
9. kilometres	ki. km. klm.	10. kilograms	ki. km. kg.
11. litres	L. lr. li.	12. millilitres	Ml. ml. Mi.
13. Sunday	Su. Snd. Sun.	14. Monday	Mo. Mdy. Mon.
15. Tuesday	Tues. Ts. Tu.	16. Wednesday	Wedn. We. Wed.
17. Thursday	Th. Thurs. Thdy	18. Friday	Fri. Frd. Fry
19. Saturday	Sat. Sa. Sdy.	20. January	Jan. Janu. Jnry.
21. February	Febr. Fbry. Feb.	22. March	Mch. Ma. Mar.
23. April	Apr. Ap. Al.	24. May	May My. Ma.
25. June	Jun. June Jn.	26. July	Jul. Jy. Ju.
27. August	Aug. Au. Aust.	28. September	Sept. Sep. Septe.
29. October	Oct. Octob. Oc.	30. November	Nov. Novem. No.
31. December	Decm. Dec. Dbr.	32. year	y. ye. yr.

Quotation Marks

1. Use quotation marks to show a direct quotation. A direct quotation is the exact words spoken by someone else. Place the quotation marks at the beginning and end of the quotation and include the final punctuation with the quotation.

   Example: John asked, **"How are you feeling today?"**

   Note: (1) a comma is placed after "asked" to set off the quotation

   (2) the quotation includes only the words spoken by John

   (3) the final punctuation, the question mark, is placed inside the quotation marks

   An indirect quotation sometimes referred to as a **paraphrase** does not require quotation marks because either it does not refer to the exact words or it is not set off on its own.

   Examples: Indirect quotation: John asked me how I was feeling.

   Direct quotation: John asked, **"How are you feeling today?"**

2. Use quotation marks around titles of poems, plays, short stories, television programmes, film titles, songs, or titles of magazine articles.

   Examples: Shakespeare wrote **"Romeo and Juliet"**.

   I read Morley Callaghan's story **"A Cap For Steve"**.

   "Yesterday" by the Beatles is one of the most popular songs of all time.

Exercise D

Place quotation marks where necessary and add commas to set off quotations. Add other punctuation marks where necessary.

1. She said Please help me lift the boxes.

2. What time is it he asked.

3. I read the short story A Monkey's Paw by W.W. Jacobs.

4. We found travel information in the magazine article Skiing in the Rockies.

5. The teacher stated Homework is due for tomorrow.

6. The movie The Wizard of Oz is a family favourite.

7. Where are you going for your summer holidays asked our teacher.

8. We were singing along to Happy Birthday to You at the party.

9. Don't you know the answer asked Teddy

10. Last Christmas by George Michael is a nice song.

11. Can you tell me who wrote Julius Caesar?

14 Tips for Effective Writing

> **Wordiness**
>
> One simple rule of effective writing is to keep sentences simple and easy to understand. Some students use unnecessary, extra words to make a simple statement.
>
> This writing problem is also referred to as "padded language".
>
> **Example**: He was late due to the fact that the bus failed to arrive on time.
>
> **Correction**: He was late because the bus was late.

Exercise A

In each of the following sentences, replace the wordy phrase with a simple word from the word bank below.

before	now	often	because
until	think	by	although

1. He will wait until such time as the train arrives.

   _____

2. They travelled across Canada by means of a car.

   _____

3. Prior to the time of the game, no fans had arrived.

   _____

4. I am of the opinion that she should be chosen as the class representative.

   _____

5. At this point in time we will leave for school.

   _____

6. Due to the fact that it was his birthday, there was a big party.

   _____

7. He would on many occasions walk to school alone.

   _____

8. In spite of the fact that he won the race, he was still not happy.

   _____

Homonym Errors

Homonyms are words that sound the same but are spelled differently.

It is easy to confuse words that sound the same when writing a sentence.

Example: She couldn't find a thing to **where** to the party.

Correction: She couldn't find a thing to **wear** to the party.

Exercise B

Find the incorrect word usages in the sentences below and replace them with the proper words.

One of the sentences below has two incorrect word usages.

1. She was so happy that she had past all her subjects.

_____

2. He ate the hole pie all by himself.

_____

3. In there backyard, they planted a pair tree.

_____

4. The man with a blue tie is my principle.

_____

5. For her birthday, she received many presence.

_____

6. This is the last weak of school before the holidays.

_____

7. Who's dog is barking?

_____

8. The game was cancelled because of bad whether.

_____

9. Its too late to make a change in our science project.

_____

10. They worked hard for they're spending money.

_____

Choppy Sentences

Sometimes short sentences can be effective. However, short, choppy sentences can be tiresome for the reader, and fail to build the idea sufficiently that the writer is trying to create.

Example (1): effective short sentence – It was the best time of my life.

A sentence like the one above needs to be brief to capture the importance of a single idea.

Example (2): It was a cold night. It was also windy. I decided to stay home.

These sentences should be combined to read:
Because it was a cold and windy night, I decided to stay home.

Exercise C

Combine each group of choppy sentences into one sentence. Write the revised sentence in the space provided.

1. John has skates. They are new. They were very expensive.

   _____

2. George has a job. He works part-time. He works part-time at the variety store.

   _____

3. The rain stopped. The sun came out. We continued to play the game.

   _____

4. He was the top student. He won the award. The award was given at an assembly.

   _____

5. Barbados is an island. It is a coral island. It is in the Caribbean.

   _____

6. Toronto is a large city. The population of Toronto is nearly three million.

   _____

7. The house was brick. The house had a swimming pool. The house was large.

   _____

8. Kara is a student. She attends the high school. The high school has 1,100 students.

   _____

9. The boy is tall. The boy is thin. He is rushing out of the room. The room is dark. The room is stuffy.

   _____

Double Negatives

When a negative statement involves two negative words, a double negative occurs. There should be only one negative word for each negative statement.

Example(1): He doesn't have no money.
Correction: He doesn't have any money.

Example(2): Lorraine can't hardly wait for the holidays.
Correction: Lorraine can hardly wait for the holidays.

Exercise D

Spot the double negative in each sentence. Correct the sentence and write the corrected version in the space provided.

> The negative terms are italicized. Remember, only use one negative term for each negative statement.

1. The teacher *didn't* have *no* chalk left.

   _____

2. Ian told Gerry that it *wasn't none* of his business.

   _____

3. Amanda *can't* tell *nobody* about what happened.

   _____

4. "*Don't* give me *no* more work to do," he exclaimed.

   _____

5. She *didn't* have *no* idea what time it was.

   _____

6. I *can't* find *nothing* in the drawer.

   _____

7. The children *weren't* going *nowhere* after school.

   _____

8. "*Don't* do *nothing* for the time being," he said.

   _____

15 The Descriptive Paragraph

Spatial Order

Imagine a place that you are familiar with and think of the position of objects in that place. Now, think of descriptive words (colour, size, shape, texture, positioning) that could be used to describe these objects. When you describe the place focusing on these objects in the order that they appear, you are using spatial order as a means of composing a description.

Think of a camera panning a room. The details of that room would appear on camera in the order that they appear in the room, and the details of those objects would be visible to the camera.

Exercise A

Choose a room in your home that you would like to describe. Pretend you are a camera moving around the room. Describe, in detail, objects in the room.

Make sure that you are describing details in the order they appear. Remember to introduce your paragraph with a topic sentence that tells the reader what you are about to describe.

HINTS:
1. Use words and phrases such as over, under, beneath, on top of, beside, next to, which will give exact details about the position of your objects.
2. Try to use at least one descriptive word for each object you describe (colour, size, shape, texture).

Title: _____

Topic sentence: _____

_____

_____

_____

_____

_____

_____

The Narrative Paragraph

A narrative paragraph is one that basically tells a story – the relating of events that have happened. Narrative paragraphs might include detailed descriptions, but their purpose is to entertain by telling a story.

Chronological Order

Chronological order refers to the telling of events in the order in which they happen according to time. This method is most often used when writing a narrative paragraph.

If, for example, you choose to write a story about a holiday event, you might follow this order of narration:

1. describe preparations for your trip
2. tell of events during your travel
3. describe your destination upon arrival
4. tell of an event that happened while at your holiday destination
5. describe your return trip home

Exercise B

Compose a narrative paragraph outlining an event that happened to you. Present the details of this event in the order in which they happened according to time. Use as many descriptive details as possible to help the reader visualize the details of your story.

It is often easier to write about an event that actually happened to you.

Title: _____

Topic sentence: _____

_____

_____

_____

_____

_____

_____

_____

_____

_____

The Explanatory Paragraph

The purpose of an explanatory paragraph is to give a detailed explanation of the way something is done. Often in an explanatory paragraph, the method is to explain a process, step by step.

If, for example, you are explaining how to do something, then the logical thing to do is to use chronological (time sequence) order – that is, the order in which things should be done.

You may use transitional words such as: next, then, when, after, afterwards.

Exercise C

Choose a task that you can explain. Give a step-by-step, detailed explanation from start to finish of exactly how to complete the task.

Suggested Topics

Learning How to Skate	Building a Snow Fort
Loading a Computer Game	Building a Backyard Rink
Creating a Piece of Art	Baking a Cake

Title: _____

Topic sentence: _____

_____ .

_____

_____

_____

_____

_____

_____

_____

_____

_____

_____

_____

_____

_____

_____

Letter Writing

Letters are usually classified as either **business** or **friendly**.

The friendly letter consists of the following parts:

1. A heading: the address of the person you are writing to
2. Salutation: an opening greeting (usually Dear...)
3. Body: the text of the letter
4. Closing: usually Yours truly or sincerely
5. Signature

Example Format:

1 33 Briar Hill Road,
Toronto, Ontario,
M4E 2L6

Date:

2 Dear Paul,

3

4 Yours truly,

5

Exercise D

Write a letter to a friend, relative, or family member telling of an event or describing something.

Dear _____,

_____

_____

_____

_____

_____

_____,

Progress Test 2

Verbals

Exercise A

State the part of speech for each underlined verbal in the following sentences. Circle your answer from the three choices.

1. <u>Walking</u> is good exercise.

   | noun | adjective | adverb |

2. <u>To speak</u> in public can be frightening.

   | noun | adjective | adverb |

3. The horse trotted up to the <u>watering</u> hole.

   | noun | adjective | adverb |

4. He discovered the <u>lost</u> treasure.

   | noun | adjective | adverb |

5. She loved <u>to skate</u> on the frozen lake.

   | noun | adjective | adverb |

6. Uncle Nike has repaired the <u>broken</u> vase.

   | noun | adjective | adverb |

Participle Phrases

Exercise B

> A participle phrase acts as an adjective in a sentence. It consists of a participle and its associated words.

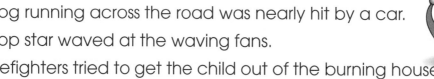

Underline the participle phrase in each sentence below.

1. The garden was filled with flowers.
2. People waiting for the bus were getting impatient.
3. Laughing at the clown, the children were entertained.
4. The dog running across the road was nearly hit by a car.
5. The pop star waved at the waving fans.
6. The firefighters tried to get the child out of the burning house.

Exercise C

Complete each of the following sentences with a verbal of your choice.

1. _____ is good exercise.

2. He wanted _____ new hockey equipment.

3. She bought _____ paper from the stationery store.

4. The children enjoy _____ on the swings.

5. _____ with a friend is fun.

6. Their house had a large _____ area on the main floor.

7. The gifts were _____ in the cupboard.

8. The boy wanted _____ a professional athlete when he grew up.

Sentence Structure

Exercise D

Correct the run-on sentences by doing one of the following:

1. **add proper punctuation**
2. **change the sentence into two sentences**
3. **change one of the independent clauses to a dependent (subordinate) clause.**

Change the wording of a sentence if it corrects the run-on problem and clarifies the meaning.

1. Don't ask questions you should listen to all the information first.

   _____

2. We woke up early packed our bags jumped in the car and left.

   _____

3. The students went to the zoo they saw exotic animals it was a great day.

   _____

4. The circus came to town they had many great acts we enjoyed them.

   _____

5. Boys play basketball girls play volleyball they do these activities at recess.

   _____

Progress Test 2

Sentence Combining

Exercise E

Combine each short sentence grouping into one sentence.

> Some sentences can be converted to single word adjectives. Often a conjunction (and, or, but) is useful for combining short sentences.

1. The students were hungry. The students ate lunch. The students ate in the park.

   _____

2. The dog barked. The dog barked at the mailman. The mailman was friendly.

   _____

3. The night came. The night was cold. The wind blew.

   _____

4. Susan was a new student. She was new to our school. She came to school today.

   _____

5. Hockey is a popular sport. Hockey is popular in Canada.

   _____

Punctuation

> There are four kinds of sentences: declarative, imperative, interrogative, and exclamatory.

Exercise F

Identify the sentence type and place the proper punctuation at the end of each sentence.

1. What time is it   _____
2. Look out   _____
3. I am taking my dog for a walk   _____
4. You don't play chess, do you   _____
5. Stay where you are   _____
6. Don't you touch my drawing   _____
7. Have you ever been to Banff   _____

Contractions

Exercise G

Fill in the chart with the proper contractions.

Expanded Form	Contraction	Expanded Form	Contraction
1. will not	_____	2. did not	_____
3. has not	_____	4. we are	_____
5. she has	_____	6. we have	_____
7. cannot	_____	8. could not	_____
9. was not	_____	10. they are	_____
11. I am	_____	12. he is	_____
13. it is	_____	14. do not	_____

Colons and Semicolons

Exercise H

In each space provided, enter a colon or a semicolon.

1. The following were needed for the party __ paper plates, drinks, hot dogs, and cake.

2. The train arrived from Montreal __ it was full of French speaking passengers.

3. The hockey game went into overtime __ suddenly, John scored the winning goal.

4. The teacher had just one request __ the hard work of his students.

5. At 3 __ 30 pm the bell will ring __ we will be dismissed from school.

6. It was 12 __ 45 and we were hungry __ thankfully, lunch was finally served.

7. He witnessed the most beautiful sight __ the sunset over the ocean.

8. They were exhausted from the long walk __ a soak in a hot tub was welcome.

Progress Test 2

Possessives

Exercise I

Circle the correct possessive form of the nouns below.

1. people   peoples' people's
2. her   her's hers
3. Louis   Louis' Louis's
4. doctors   doctors' doctor's
5. player   player's players'
6. players   players' players's
7. class   class's class'
8. men   mens' men's

Comma Use

> The number in parentheses tells you the number of commas missing in each sentence.

Exercise J

Add the comma(s) needed in each sentence below.

1. On July 10 2003 they will celebrate an anniversary and go out for dinner. (2)
2. Although they were the first to arrive no one noticed them. (1)
3. Jeff asked "Is the appointment for August 2 2002 or is it for a later date?" (3)
4. The tool kit included: a wrench a hammer nails and a screwdriver. (3)
5. Unless you change the time no one will be able to attend the meeting. (1)
6. Hammerhead Peter's bulldog is very playful in spite of his fierce look. (2)

Quotation Marks

Exercise K

Place quotation marks where needed in the following sentences.

1. Sam asked, Who will be on my team?
2. We went to see Beauty and the Beast.
3. We sang Happy Birthday to You.
4. Sasha stated, I don't think I can go swimming today.
5. Our class read the short story A Day on the Farm.
6. We could have won the game, said the dejected captain.

Apostrophes

The number at the end of the sentence in parentheses indicates how many apostrophes are missing.

Exercise L

In each sentence below, add the missing apostrophe(s).

1. Hes the best player on our team but he doesnt know it. (2)

2. He borrowed Pauls book and hasnt returned it yet. (2)

3. Its about time you took your dog to get its new collar. (1)

4. When its time to go, youll know it. (2)

5. He wasnt always a student at our school; he arrived in 99. (2)

Exercise M

Re-write the following paragraph adding the missing punctuation marks.

The Grade six students were looking eagerly forward to Friday Ms Patterson their teacher promised to take them to the Science Centre However the children had to do some research first You should work in groups of three or four and each group has to find the information on this worksheet explained Ms Patterson Can we get it from the Internet asked Jenny Sure answered Ms Patterson but you must double check the information because not all the information on the Net is accurate

_____

_____

_____

_____

_____

Vocabulary & Usage

1 | The Topic Sentence

A **topic sentence** introduces the main idea of a paragraph. Topic sentences must be focused enough to let the reader know what the paragraph is about.

A. **Circle the letter of the most appropriate topic sentence from each group below.**

Base your selection on the following criteria:
a.   creates interest for the reader
b.   gives sufficient information or direction as to what is being written about
c.   gives a more focused topic

1) The Storm

A.   It was a stormy night.

B.   Dark clouds covered the sky.

C.   When we saw the storm coming, we made the necessary preparations to protect ourselves.

2) The Final Game

A.   The score in the final game was close.

B.   With the score tied and minutes left to play in the final game, the unthinkable happened.

C.   No one was ready for what happened during the final game.

3) The New Family Pet

A.   Our friends and neighbours were shocked when they first saw the new family pet we brought home.

B.   Every family should have a new pet every now and then.

C.   Some animals make ideal family pets.

4) The Greatest Show on Earth

A.   The Cirque du Soleil provided the greatest night of entertainment our family had ever experienced.

B.   Everyone enjoys the circus.

C.   Our family went to the circus for the first time.

Composing Topic Sentences

B. Compose an interesting and informative topic sentence for each paragraph below. Add a title for each paragraph.

Paragraph 1 Title: _____

Topic Sentence: _____

_____ .

The hotel we stayed at was located right on the beach. Every day after breakfast, we would cool off in the clear, warm water of the Atlantic. In the afternoons, we often played tennis on the courts next to the hotel or miniature golf at the play centre across the road. Everyone was so pleased with the holiday that we decided to return next year.

Paragraph 2 Title: _____

Topic Sentence: _____

_____ .

Just before the race was to begin, our best runner, Lauren, got a cramp in her side. She was doubled up in pain and was unable to compete. Our hopes of winning the 200-metre race disappeared. Suddenly, she stood up and, despite the discomfort of the cramp, declared that she would compete. The whole school cheered when she stepped up to the starting line.

Paragraph 3 Title: _____

Topic Sentence: _____

_____ .

Once the seat was adjusted and he took a few practice turns with the bike, he was ready for a long ride. The eighteen speeds made climbing hills easy. He rode along the lake road, through the woods, and along the bike path next to the highway. He stopped at the roadside to eat a sandwich he had packed and to take a drink of water. After riding for an hour, he turned and headed back for home. In total, he had ridden 50 kilometres on the new bike. He knew that with this bike, he could plan many more bike-riding adventures.

Composing Paragraphs

C. **Below are topic sentences. Compose a short paragraph of three or four sentences for each topic.**

1. Camping is a wonderful way to experience nature particularly if your campsite is deep in the wilderness. _____

_____

_____

_____

_____

_____

_____

2. Richard and Paul were very excited about going into grade six because they would be moving into the new building equipped with lockers and a new gymnasium. _____

_____

_____

_____

_____

_____

3. To make this picnic memorable, the group decided to pack their favourite foods including some irresistible snacks. _____

_____

_____

_____

_____

_____

> *Weak topic sentences can be improved by adding more information.*

Example: Topic sentence: Building sand sculptures is fun.
Improved topic sentence: With a shovel, a bucket, and a little imagination, there is no limit to what sand sculptures you can create.

D. Improve the following topic sentences.

1. The movie was scary.

   Improved topic sentence: _____

   _____

   _____

2. My cousins arrived today from Italy.

   Improved topic sentence: _____

   _____

3. The sky went black.

   Improved topic sentence: _____

   _____

   _____

4. Today was our moving day.

   Improved topic sentence: _____

   _____

5. Today we were having a science test.

   Improved topic sentence: _____

   _____

   _____

6. We learned an important lesson that day.

   Improved topic sentence: _____

   _____

2 Following the Topic Sentence

A. For each topic sentence below, add two or three more sentences to make a complete paragraph. The sentences you create should further develop the topic sentence.

1. In the middle of the night, I heard a strange noise outside my bedroom window.

_____

_____

_____

_____

_____

_____

2. The pilot announced over the speaker that we should fasten our seatbelts because we were in for a rough landing.

_____

_____

_____

_____

_____

_____

3. The package addressed to me was delivered by courier, and when I opened it, I was shocked.

_____

_____

_____

_____

_____

Creating Paragraphs

B. Create a paragraph of three or four sentences using as many words in each group as possible.

A **paragraph** is a group of sentences that are closely related in topic.

moon	trees	campsite	bears
wind	noises	fire	twigs	scary
campfire	tent	lantern	breakfast
leader	stars	sleeping	stories	woods
leaves	sleeping bags	snoring	laughter
marshmallows	porridge	darkness	

Title: _____

_____

_____

_____

_____

_____

_____

_____

_____

_____

_____

party	friends	surprise	balloons	cake	afternoon
ice cream	gifts			hiding	lights
darkness	candles			funny	games
singing	music			parents	winners
home	food			spilled	cards
Saturday	bowling			strike	noisy

Title: _____

_____

_____

_____

_____

_____

_____

_____

_____

_____

_____

_____

_____

C. **Write a topic sentence for each short paragraph below. The topic sentence should introduce the main idea of the paragraph.**

1. _____

   _____

   We had never been on a cruise ship before and we were very excited. When the ship blasted its horn and pulled away, we stood on the deck and waved at the people on the pier even though we didn't know them. We were on our way to visit six Caribbean islands in seven days at sea.

2. _____
_____

The line up for rides were long and it was very hot outside. Luckily, we had brought bottles of water with us. Finally, it was our turn to board the ride and each one of us was scared stiff.

3. _____
_____

He approached the free throw line and bounced the ball a few times to set himself. The crowd behind the basket tried to distract him but he concentrated on the rim. The ball went up rotating in the air. It landed on the rim, bounced, spun, wavered, wobbled, and finally fell through the hoop.

4. _____
_____

The puppy ran around the house, sliding on the hardwood floors and bumping into the dining room chairs. He ran under the table and began tugging on the loose table cloth. Training this little monster was going to be a big job.

5. _____
_____

The trainer showed us a number of horses and asked us to choose the one we would like to ride. After we got in the saddle, our guide began leading us in a slow trot. Then, we broke into a mild gallop and suddenly horseback riding became thrilling.

3 Descriptive Language (1)

To make your writing more interesting and meaningful, try using more descriptive words for the things you are writing about. Some words are more descriptive than others although they may have similar meaning.

A. **For each sentence, underline the most appropriate word to replace the italicized word.**

1. They rested in the ski *building*.

   lodge   home   tower   apartment

2. The *big house* had twelve bedrooms and three living rooms.

   chalet   mansion   residence   dwelling

3. The *loud* dog growled at the postman.

   careful   ferocious   rude   unhappy

4. She read a *good* book.

   interesting   thick   short   long

5. They laughed at the *man who told jokes on stage*.

   actor   entertainer   comedian   singer

6. The *tall* boy played basketball.

   thin   slight   lofty   lanky

7. He bought a shiny, new, red *vehicle*.

   car   automobile   convertible   auto

8. The *building* flashed a light to warn sailors.

   tower   structure   lighthouse   skyscraper

9. The *athlete* prepared for the race.

   professional   sprinter   runner   jogger

10. They enjoyed a *nice* meal at the new restaurant.

    hot   unusual   juicy   gourmet

Action Verbs

Use an action verb to give the reader a better understanding of what is actually happening in the sentence. Consider the context of each sentence.

Example: 1. He <u>went</u> down the ice towards the net.
2. He **roared** down the ice towards the net.

B. From the list of verbs below each sentence, underline the best replacement for the italicized verb.

1. He *walked* down the street slowly.

   sauntered   ran   hopped   glided

2. They *went* home to get money before the show started.

   strolled   rushed   drifted   arrived

3. The dog *jumped up* in the air to catch the Frisbee.

   leaped   rose   bounced   elevated

4. The bird *came* down out of the sky to catch the fish.

   dropped   flew   swooped   slipped

5. He *skated* around the defensemen and scored a goal.

   circled   zigzagged   squeezed   slid

6. The door *shut* from a sudden gust of wind through the house.

   closed   locked   swung   slammed

7. The sailboat *moved* lazily in the breeze.

   drifted   sailed   roared   travelled

8. Lightning *was seen* across the black sky.

   slashed   screamed   flashed   sparked

9. The sun *shone* down on the sunbathers on the beach.

   lit   sprayed   touched   blazed

10. The lion *ate* the huge hunks of raw meat.

   consumed   devoured   had   enjoyed

Understanding Meaning through Context

C. Match the underlined words with the meanings listed below. Use the context to determine the meaning of the underlined words.

The <u>sleek</u> sailboat <u>floated</u> <u>gingerly</u> across the <u>undulating</u> water. The bright sails billowed in the breeze as the bow dipped <u>gracefully</u> in and out of the waves. A <u>refreshing</u> spray of water splashed upon the slippery deck.

The captain announced a warning to the crew, cautioning them about the <u>precarious</u> condition of the wet deck. Suddenly, one of the crew <u>shrieked</u> before <u>careening</u> backwards into the lake. The captain <u>roared</u>, "Man overboard!" <u>Efficiently</u> the crew <u>executed</u> an <u>instantaneous</u> rescue. The <u>voyage</u> continued without further <u>complications</u>.

1. immediate _____

2. carefully, cautiously _____

3. spoke loudly, yelled _____

4. trip, tour _____

5. dangerous, threatening _____

6. cool, fresh _____

7. slim, narrow, streamlined _____

8. performed, made happen _____

9. difficulties, problems _____

10. curving, wavy _____

11. performed with skill, expertly _____

12. bobbed, drifted, stayed above water _____

13. gently, easily, smoothly, with control _____

14. leaning, tilting _____

15. screamed, screeched, howled _____

Creating Adjectives from Verbs

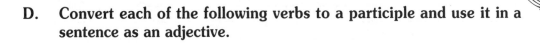

A **participle** is an adjective form of a verb.

Example: verb – walk
            adjective form – walking
            The old man used a **walking** stick for balance.

D. Convert each of the following verbs to a participle and use it in a sentence as an adjective.

1. sing

   _____

2. dine

   _____

3. run

   _____

4. cry

   _____

5. speak

   _____

6. fish

   _____

7. swim

   _____

8. drive

   _____

9. burn

   _____

10. fall

   _____

4 Confusing Words

Frequently Misspelled Words

A. Circle the correct spelling from the choices for each of these frequently misspelled words.

> *If you are unsure, use your dictionary.*

1.	noticeable	noticeble	noticable
2.	defenite	definate	definite
3.	sucess	success	succes
4.	heros	heroes	heross
5.	occurrence	ocurrence	occurence
6.	neccessary	necesary	necessary
7.	receive	recive	recieve
8.	therefor	therefour	therefore
9.	professer	profesor	professor
10.	arguement	argument	argament

Working with Homonyms

Homonyms are words that sound alike but have different meanings.

Examples: "whether" and "weather"

He asked **whether** or not I was going to school today because the **weather** forecast called for a storm.

B. Circle the correct word to suit the meaning (context) of each sentence below.

1. They waited for there / their ride home after school.

2. She received many presence / presents for her birthday.

3. The dog dug a hole / whole in which to bury its bone.

4. She was very sad when her fish past / passed away.

5. " Whose / Who's in charge?" she inquired.

6. The ship sailed out of site / sight into the sunset.

7. Because he hadn't eaten, he felt week / weak .

8. The enemies fought a duel / dual with swords.

9. She came forth / fourth in the 100-metre sprint.

10. The wobbly bicycle wheel was loose / lose .

11. The tailor will alter / altar his suit.

12. The campers worried about a bear / bare in the woods.

13. He had a heavy load to bear / bare .

14. The herd / heard of elephants stopped by the river for a drink.

15. The doctor had many patience / patients in his waiting room.

16. The principle / principal of the school visited the classrooms.

17. The plane / plain was forced to land on the open plane / plain .

18. The council / counsel will give council / counsel to the recruits.

19. Because he had a cold, his voice was hoarse / horse .

20. She wrote in her dairy / diary the events of her holiday.

21. They paid their fare / fair to go to the fare / fair .

22. She took a coffee break / brake in the morning only.

23. The soldiers were there to keep the peace / piece .

24. Geography was his favourite school coarse / course .

25. They were bored / board with the movie they were watching.

Tricky Usage Problems

this   that   them   these   those

"This" and "that" modify single nouns.
"Them", "these", and "those" modify plural nouns.

Note 1:   "Those" may be either an adjective or a pronoun.
           "Them" is always a pronoun and never an adjective.
Note 2:   Words such as "type of", "sort of", and "kind of" are treated as singular.

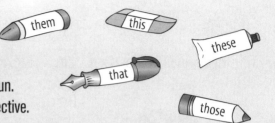

C.   Circle the correct word for each sentence.

1.   She chose this / these sort of book to read on the train.

2.   He put these / them clothes in the dresser.

3.   This / Them type of game is very challenging.

4.   That / Those types of people are fun to be with.

5.   She preferred to sing this / those kind of song.

6.   He is happy with that / these types of activity.

7.   This / Those kinds of sports are dangerous.

8.   She called them / those on the telephone.

9.   Those / That kind of pizza was his favourite.

More Tricky Usage

good   bad   badly   well

"Good" should be used only as an adjective.

Example: He had a **good** time at the party.
Incorrect: She did not feel **good**.
Correct: She did not feel **well**.

"Bad" is used after a linking verb.

Example: She felt **bad** about missing the rehearsal.

"Badly" is used after an action verb.

Example: He played **badly** in the final game.

"Well" is used after an action verb.

Example: He played **well** in the final game.
Incorrect: He played **good** in the final game.

D. Write the correct word in the space provided.

1. The coach felt _____ about the team's victory.

good / well

2. The food tastes _____ because it was not refrigerated.

bad / badly

3. She was _____ at being a soccer goalkeeper.

good / well

4. He felt _____ about the news that he was moving away.

bad / badly

5. She sang _____ because she had a sore throat.

bad / badly

6. He felt _____ after a long rest in bed.

good / well

"Fewer" and "Less"

"Fewer" refers to an exact number; "less" refers to an amount or quantity.

Incorrect: There were **less** people in the audience.
Correct: There were **fewer** people in the audience

Incorrect: He drank **less** bottles of water than he needed.
Correct: He drank **fewer** bottles of water than he needed.

E.   Circle the correct term for each sentence.

1. She had written (fewer / less) words in her story than required.

2. He drank (fewer / less) milk than he did when he was younger.

3. (Less / Fewer) people are taking public transit than predicted.

4. There were (fewer / less) cases of influenza this past winter.

5. As the expression goes: (less / fewer) is more.

6. The teacher had (less / fewer) concerns because the students all did well.

5 Creating a Story Ending

A story is often made up of a conflict or a situation that needs to be solved. A story ending is the part of the story where the problem or conflict is finally solved. Often, suspense or a series of events is used to build towards a story ending.

A. Below is a story about a track and field event. Provide an ending paragraph for the story in the space provided. Add a title that suits your ending.

Title: _____

The mid-June day of the final track and field meet was met by temperatures approaching 30°C. The air was still and the scorching sun blazed down on the competitors who huddled under the sparse trees for shade. Litres of water were being consumed by the athletes before competing. Some just poured the water over their heads in a vain attempt at momentary relief.

Lisa, an 11-year-old sprinter, was the one hope her school had of bringing home a ribbon. She specialized in the 200-metre race, a race that demanded endurance and strategy. Small in size, she was big in heart, and her legs were like pistons pumping fiercely when she ran. Lisa had placed first in the divisional race and second in the regional where she was defeated by a mere 2 seconds by her main competitor, another 11-year-old runner named Jennifer. Jennifer was a tall girl with long legs that enabled her to run in steady, loping strides. Both runners were fierce competitors and superb athletes. Both were determined to win.

The announcement came for the 200-metre final – runners were asked to report to the starter. There was a swell of spectators gathering at the finish line anticipating a spectacular finish. Lisa and Jennifer set themselves into the starting blocks staring straight ahead. They arched their backs and lowered their heads. The starter raised the pistol, and at the sound of the shot, they were off – the championship race was on.

30 metres into the race, Lisa and Jennifer, neck and neck, had jumped out to an insurmountable lead over the other runners. The rest of the field were now

racing for third place as they watched the pair of runners round the first turn and speed down the straight-way. The crowd cheered wildly. At the 100-metre mark, Lisa had taken a slight lead but Jennifer stayed just off her right shoulder waiting to make her move.

At 160 metres, the runners were again neck and neck, well ahead of the pack. Then the unthinkable happened. Lisa soared into the lead, but as she sprinted ahead, she stumbled and sprawled to the ground. The crowd was silenced.

_____

_____

_____

_____

_____

_____

_____

_____

_____

_____

_____

_____

The Parts of a Story

Setting

The setting of a story refers to the time and place in which the story takes place.

B.   State two facts about the setting that are known to the reader immediately.

1. _____

2. _____

Characters

Characters in a story can be divided into two basic categories:

(a) **Major characters:** They are usually directly involved in the action or conflict.

(b) **Minor characters:** They have limited involvement in the story; sometimes they deliver messages or interact with the major characters to help move the story along.

C.   Who are the major and minor characters in this story?

Major: _____

Minor: _____

Descriptions

A writer will use descriptions to help the reader visualize the setting, the characters, and the action in the story.

D.   State four descriptions that you think are effective.

1. _____

2. _____

3. _____

4. _____

Plot

Plot refers to the main action that takes place in the story. The plot usually follows a path of development from beginning to end.

E.   Describe the plot of this story.

_____

_____

_____

Conflict

Conflict often forms the basis of a story. It may involve two persons against each other, a character fighting against himself/herself (decision making), or a character facing nature.

F.   State the central conflict in this story.

_____

_____

_____

Suspense

Suspense is a technique of writing that "suspends" the reader by holding back information or by giving only partial information to build the ending.

G.   Describe the suspense in this story.

_____

_____

_____

H.   Is the suspense effective? Explain why or why not.

_____

_____

_____

6 Word-Building Challenge

Your vocabulary can be expanded by developing new words from a root word.

A. Build a series of words from the root word given (Try adding a prefix or suffix). Then circle the best synonym from the choices given.

A new synonym to add to your vocabulary is given with each question below.

Example:

decide (verb)	Words developed:	decision	decisive

Synonym: (choose) review think list

New synonym: *resolve* (to solve an issue)

---

1. **engage** _____ _____

   Synonym: trap fix occupy engulf

   New synonym: *monopolize* (to control, engage fully)

---

2. **occur** _____ _____

   Synonym: complete happen try effect

   New synonym: *transpire* (to take place)

---

3. **rage** _____ _____

   Synonym: feelings attitude hate fury

   New synonym: *fad* (something that becomes popular)

---

4. **produce** _____ _____

   Synonym: make repair apply destroy

   New synonym: *yield* (to produce as in crops)

5.	**neglect**	_____ _____
	Synonym:	hide disappear ignore refuse
	New synonym:	*omit* (to leave out)

6.	**identity**	_____ _____
	Synonym	self search dental imagine
	New synonym:	*individuality* (personal characteristics that set a person apart from others)

B. **Place each new word in the sentence below that suits its meaning.**

monopolize   transpire   fad

yield   omit   individuality

1. The hula-hoop _____ took place in the 1960's.

2. We must be proud of our _____ because it is who we are.

3. If you _____ too many answers on the test, you may not pass.

4. They will wait to see what will _____ over the next few days before they make a decision.

5. The farmer was happy with the _____ from the farm this year.

6. He always tries to _____ the conversation by talking too much.

New Words in Context

C. **Circle a suitable synonym for the underlined word in each sentence below.**

> These words may be new to you. Use the meaning (context) of the sentence to help you define the words.

1. The pain in his knee was <u>tolerable</u> so he was able to continue to run.

   bearable   painful   slight   severe

2. It was a <u>momentous</u> occasion when he received the Most Valuable Player Award.

   useless   boring   important   critical

3. The <u>incompetent</u> driver caused the accident.

   skilled   equipped   incapable   tricky

4. The <u>repulsive</u> monster in the horror movie frightened the audience.

   huge   disgusting   aggressive   sleepy

5. The <u>prominent</u> citizen was popular with the residents of the town.

   dangerous   happy   serious   well-known

6. The <u>obstinate</u> student refused to admit his answer was wrong even though there was proof.

   stubborn   intelligent   careful   sneaky

7. The <u>laborious</u> task of digging the trench tired out even the young workers.

   simple   interesting   difficult   creative

8. It was <u>hazardous</u> driving through the storm at night.

   easy   uneventful   dangerous   amusing

9. He had an <u>extraordinary</u> experience watching the whales off the Gaspé Peninsula.

   boring   frightful   incredible   useful

10. The injured animal was a <u>pathetic</u> sight.

    unusual   pitiful   strange   powerful

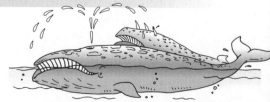

Homonym Challenge

D. Write the homonyms using the clues.

> A **homonym** is a word that sounds the same as another word but has a different meaning.

1. (a) look at

   st _____

   (b) climb one at a time

   st _____

2. (a) centre of apple

   co _____

   (b) army troops

   co _____

3. (a) holes in skin

   po _____

   (b) dispenses a liquid

   po _____

4. (a) to come apart

   br _____

   (b) to stop

   br _____

5. (a) bright colour

   r _____

   (b) book activity

   r _____

6. (a) end of day

   n _____

   (b) in King Arthur's Court

   k _____

7. (a) to be permitted

   al _____

   (b) to speak so all can hear

   al _____

8. (a) falls from clouds

   r _____

   (b) a king's rule

   r _____

9. (a) direction to go

   w _____

   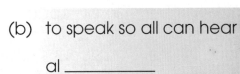

   (b) measure heaviness

   w _____

10. (a) float on water

   sa _____

   (b) reduced price

   sa _____

7 | Descriptive Language (2)

Descriptive language helps the reader establish a clear picture of what you are describing. In creative writing, it is important to choose words that are precise and colourful.

A. Circle the descriptive word below each sentence that would be a suitable replacement for the italicized word. Choose the one that best fits the context of the sentence.

1. The *awful* road conditions made driving impossible.

   hazardous   smooth   bumpy   tight

2. The students were *happy* that their team won the final game.

   concerned   upset   glad   excited

3. Their new house was so *big* that they had to buy more furniture.

   wide   high   spacious   cramped

4. The creature in the film was so *awful* they couldn't face the screen.

   large   hideous   clever   enormous

5. The homework was so *terrible* that few students completed the work.

   entertaining   challenging   important   necessary

6. At the zoo, they watched the tiger *walk* back and forth in its cage.

   stroll   scamper   skip   pace

7. The noise from the musical instruments was *loud* for the people sitting close to the stage.

   deafening   enjoyable   clear   smooth

8. The surfers *went* over the waves with amazing balance.

   splashed   sunk   glided   dropped

9. The outfielder *moved* to his left to make an unbelievable catch.

   leaned   reached   dove   skipped

Words in Context

The meaning of a word can often be figured out by the context (meaning) of a sentence.

B. Read the paragraph below and match each underlined word with a synonym from the list. Use the context to help you decide which words match up.

Hosting Primary Play-Day

The grade five students were <u>enthusiastic</u> about <u>officiating</u> at the Primary Play-Day. The students had <u>devised</u> games which they <u>conceived</u> by a co-operative effort. They <u>compiled</u> prizes for all <u>participants</u> and <u>unique</u> rewards for the winners of games. The weather was <u>initially</u> unsuitable for this <u>affair</u> but <u>fortunately</u>, the sun <u>emerged</u> prior to the start of the games. Some students were so <u>exuberant</u> that they were <u>unruly</u> at times but when the games began, they <u>composed</u> themselves. The teachers <u>commented</u> that the day was an <u>enormous</u> success.

1. enthusiastic ____
2. officiating ____
3. devised ____
4. conceived ____
5. compiled ____
6. participants ____
7. unique ____
8. initially ____
9. affair ____
10. fortunately ____
11. emerged ____
12. exuberant ____
13. unruly ____
14. composed ____
15. commented ____
16. enormous ____

A.	unusual	B.	huge
C.	players	D.	luckily
E.	came out	F.	at first
G.	excited	H.	misbehaving
I.	controlled	J.	stated
K.	keen	L.	managing
M.	created	N.	planned
O.	collected	P.	event

C. **Based on the definitions and synonyms given, place each word in the sentence that best suits its meaning.**

grimace .... facial expression of pain

obscure .... difficult to see or find, cloudy

intrigued .... attracted to, interested in, fascinated by

jeering .... mocking, taunting, making rude remarks

coincidental .... happening at the same time as something else, by chance

obstinate .... stubborn, strong-minded, opinionated, firm

ornate .... decorative, showy, brightly coloured

bleak .... dreary, dull, bare

absurd .... ridiculous, unbelievable, unlikely

consecutive ..... in an order or sequence

energetic .... lively, healthy, robust

abundance ..... large quantity of, many of

cantankerous .. grouchy, mean

grievance .... complaint, objection

logical .... analytical, reasonable, proper by choice

Enter the most obvious words first; check each word as you use it.

1. Because there was an _____ of food, everyone had lots to eat.

2. The fans who were _____ the losing team were asked to leave the arena.

3. The morning weather looked _____ until the clouds lifted.

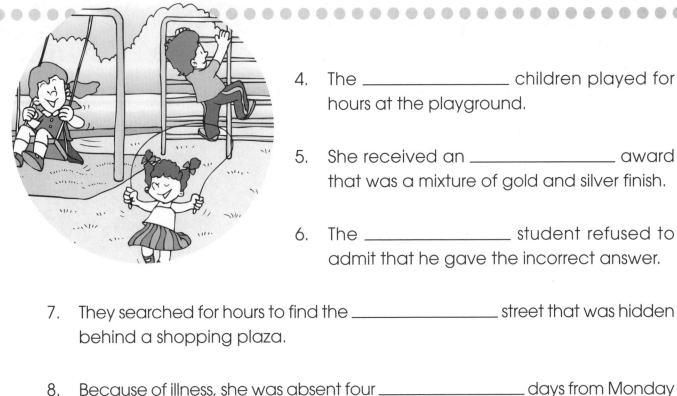

4. The _____ children played for hours at the playground.

5. She received an _____ award that was a mixture of gold and silver finish.

6. The _____ student refused to admit that he gave the incorrect answer.

7. They searched for hours to find the _____ street that was hidden behind a shopping plaza.

8. Because of illness, she was absent four _____ days from Monday to Thursday.

9. The _____ neighbour was always complaining about the children playing in front of his house.

10. Unhappy with the purchase, he issued a formal _____ to the store manager.

11. The students were _____ by the science experiment which illustrated the power of magnets.

12. It was _____ to think that they could actually buy tickets for a Toronto Maple Leafs hockey game at the Air Canada Centre.

13. It was _____ that they both were shopping in the same store at the same time.

14. The _____ on his face showed his exhaustion after the race.

15. The _____ answer was the one that appeared reasonable at first thought.

A. **Circle the best topic sentence from each group of sentences below.**

1) The Party

- A. We went to a birthday party.
- B. We went to a birthday party for Susan.
- C. Susan's surprise birthday party was planned in secret by her best friend, Lara.

2 Relatives

- A. The first time he met his relatives from Italy was when they arrived in Calgary to attend his sister's wedding.
- B. Relatives love coming to weddings.
- C. Always invite all your relatives to a wedding.

3) Raccoons

- A. Raccoons love eating garbage.
- B. Hungry raccoons are very clever at opening even the most secure garbage containers.
- C. No garbage container can stop a raccoon.

4 The Library

- A. Libraries are not just a place to get books.
- B. The library is an ideal place to do your homework because there are many resources to use and it is quiet there.
- C. If you have a homework assignment, go to the library.

5) Exercise

- A. Exercise is important for staying healthy.
- B. Regular exercise is good for people of all ages but we should never overdo it.
- C. Children, not just adults, should exercise regularly to maintain their health.

B. Match each of the words or phrases below with its more descriptive form.

1. building at a ski resort _____   A. Ferrari
2. large house   _____   B. mystery novel
3. dangerous   _____   C. comedian
4. good book   _____   D. lanky
5. funny performer   _____   E. gourmet delight
6. tall   _____   F. sprinter
7. vehicle   _____   G. ferocious
8. downtown building   _____   H. chalet
9. athlete   _____   I. mansion
10. nice meal   _____   J. skyscraper

C. Match the dull, uninteresting verbs on the left with the more vivid synonyms on the right.

1. walked (person)   _____   A. devoured
2. went in a hurry (person) _____   B. swooped
3. jumped up (animal)   _____   C. zigzagged
4. came down (bird)   _____   D. glided
5. skated (person)   _____   E. flashed
6. shut (door)   _____   F. sauntered
7. moved (sailboat)   _____   G. rushed
8. was seen (lightning)   _____   H. slammed
9. shone (sun)   _____   I. leaped
10. ate (animal)   _____   J. blazed

D.   Match each of the words with its meaning.

GROUP ONE

1. immediate _____
2. carefully _____
3. yelled _____
4. tour _____
5. dangerous _____

A. roared
B. voyage
C. precarious
D. gingerly
E. instantaneous

GROUP TWO

6.   cool, fresh _____
7.   streamlined _____
8.   performed _____
9.   difficulties _____
10. wavy _____

A. undulating
B. refreshing
C. complications
D. sleek
E. executed

GROUP THREE

11. skilfully _____
12. bobbed _____
13. smoothly _____
14. tilting _____
15. screamed _____

A. careening
B. shrieked
C. floated
D. gracefully
E. efficiently

E.   Mark each word as spelled correctly (C) or incorrectly (I). Add the corrected version.

1. noticable _____ _____
2. argument _____ _____
3. therefor _____ _____
4. neccessary _____ _____
5. recieve _____ _____

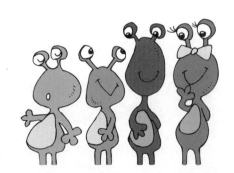

6.　heros　　　____　_____

7.　success　　____　_____

8.　definite　　____　_____

9.　professer　____　_____

10.　occurence　____　_____

F.　Underline the correct homonym in each of the sentences below.

1.　They looked for (their / there / they're) bus tickets.

2.　His (presence / presents) was expected at the meeting.

3.　(Who's / Whose) shoes were left in the hall?

4.　The (plane / plain) was full so they took the train.

5.　The (herd / heard) of cattle stampeded.

6.　The school (principal / principle) addressed the student body.

7.　She was (bored / board) with the book she was reading.

8.　The players complained that the rule change was not (fare / fair).

G.　Underline the correct word in each of the following sentences.

1.　He likes (these / this) type of car.

2.　(That / Those) types of exercises are strenuous.

3.　She did not feel (good / well) so she went home to rest.

4.　They had a (well / good) time at the fun fare.

5.　He felt (badly / bad) that he couldn't stay longer.

6.　She played (badly / bad) and lost the match.

7.　She ate (less / fewer) food than anyone else.

8.　The teacher gave (less / fewer) homework this weekend.

9.　He drank (less / fewer) cans of pop than his friend.

10.　They had (less / fewer) of a wait for the morning bus.

H. In the space provided, enter the root word for each word below.

1. decision _____

2. occurrence _____

3. outrageous _____

4. production _____

5. negligence _____

6. identification _____

I. Match the word in bold in each phrase with its synonym.

1.	**tolerable** pain	_____	A.	incapable
2.	**momentous** occasion	_____	B.	stubborn
3.	**incompetent** driver	_____	C.	bearable
4.	**repulsive** monster	_____	D.	well-known
5.	**prominent** world leader	_____	E.	important
6.	**obstinate** person	_____	F.	dangerous
7.	**laborious** task	_____	G.	incredible
8.	**hazardous** driving	_____	H.	pitiful
9.	**extraordinary** sight	_____	I.	disgusting
10.	**pathetic** mishap	_____	J.	difficult

J. Underline the synonym for each word below from the list.

1.	**hazardous**	awful	bumpy	smooth	dangerous
2.	**roomy**	spacious	hollow	wide	empty
3.	**ugly**	scary	hideous	strange	odd
4.	**difficult**	entertaining	challenging	necessary	important
5.	**loud**	entertaining	deafening	smooth	rough
6.	**glided**	splashed	dipped	crashed	floated

K. Give a homonym for each word below. Be careful to spell the homonym correctly.

1. pores – _____
2. break – _____
3. read – _____
4. night – _____
5. aloud – _____
6. rain – _____
7. weigh – _____
8. sail – _____

L. For each topic sentence below, add two or three more sentences to make a complete paragraph.

1. We had a hearty Thanksgiving dinner.

_____

_____

_____

_____

· ·

2. We were down to the last batter at the bottom of the ninth inning, trailing by one run.

_____

_____

_____

· ·

3. The courier handed me a heavy parcel.

_____

_____

_____

_____

8 The Columbia Icefield

The COLUMBIA ICEFIELD

is <u>situated</u> on the <u>boundary</u> of Jasper and Banff national parks and covers an <u>area</u> of over 325 square <u>kilometres</u>. The Icefield is made of solid ice 350 metres thick. Its melt waters feed three oceans: the Arctic, the Atlantic, and the Pacific. At the <u>base</u> of the Columbia Icefield is the Athabasca Glacier which is <u>approximately</u> 6 kilometres in length and 1 kilometre wide.

Because this glacier is easily <u>accessible</u>, tourists <u>venture</u> out onto the glacier in a specially designed vehicle called a Snocoach. The Snocoach is equipped with low pressure tires for <u>traction</u> and can transport 55 tourists to and from the centre of the Icefield. Once in the middle, the tourists can step out onto this Icefield formed from falling snow that has <u>accumulated</u> for over 400 years. To the visitor, the Columbia Icefield appears to sit perfectly still. Actually, it is in constant motion to and fro shaping the landscape. This back and forth movement takes thousands of years and is so <u>gradual</u> that it is only <u>detectable</u> through scientific research.

Although the Icefield is made up of a thick layer of ice, it is home to both plants and animals. Grizzly bears have winter dens near the Icefield and are frequently seen in the spring and fall seasons. Plants take many years to <u>establish</u> themselves in this <u>harsh</u> <u>environment</u>. To protect both the plants and animals of the area, strict rules of <u>conservation</u> are <u>enforced</u>. Tourists are asked not to feed the animals as it can actually shorten their lives. Visitors are asked to use specially <u>designed</u> footpaths to avoid trampling the plant life.

The Columbia Icefield is truly a wonder and is enjoyed by thousands of visitors each year. Hikers, campers, cyclists, and motorists take advantage of the natural beauty of the wildlife, rivers, mountains, and lakes of this <u>breath-taking</u> region.

Vocabulary Study

Re-read the passage paying particular attention to the underlined words and their meanings in context.

A. Enter the words from the passage that best suit the meanings below.

1. _____ takes place slowly, over time

2. _____ grip, friction

3. _____ rough, tough, difficult

4. _____ awesome, spectacular, wonderful

5. _____ place of nature, defined area

6. _____ easy to get to, available

7. _____ roughly, close to, near in estimate

8. _____ located, placed

9. _____ border, edge of, limit of

10. _____ built up, added up, piled up

11. _____ build, form, grow, locate, situate, put in place

12. _____ bottom, ground level

13. _____ go out into, investigate, discover

14. _____ able to be found

15. _____ applied

16. _____ drawn, formulated, built, created

17. _____ preservation, guarding wildlife

 **Working with Facts**

B. State two facts from each paragraph in the passage entitled "The Columbia Icefield".

 Paragraph **One**

1. _____

2. _____

Paragraph **Two**

1. _____

2. _____

Paragraph **Three**

1. _____

2. _____

Paragraph **Four**

1. _____

2. _____

Creating a Factual Composition

C. Read the list of facts about grizzly bears. Write a two-paragraph composition using these facts. Add your own ideas to make it interesting.

* Grizzly bears can outrun human beings.
* Grizzly bears are the largest mountain animals.
* Mountain lions are afraid of grizzly bears.
* A grizzly bear might weigh up to 230 kilograms (500 pounds).
* Grizzly bears can run up to 50 kilometres an hour.
* Grizzly bears hibernate in the winter and wake up in the spring.

- *Grizzly bears are omnivorous (they eat both plants and animals).*
- *Grizzly bears eat fish.*
- *Grizzly bears grow to be 9 feet standing upright.*
- *Grizzly bears have exceptional sense of smell, good hearing, and are powerful.*
- *Grizzly bears are shy around human beings but will attack if their food or young are threatened.*
- *Never run away from a bear; give way by backing up slowly.*
- *Never surprise a bear; always make noises to let it know you're nearby.*
- *Store food safely at your campsite.*

Choose the facts from the list above that you want to use in your composition. Organize ideas that are common into the same paragraph.

_____

_____

_____

_____

_____

_____

_____

_____

_____

_____

_____

_____

_____

_____

_____

9 Haiku Poetry

Haiku is a Japanese form of poetry that is highly descriptive. It often deals with single ideas, descriptions, or moments. The standard format is three lines with a total number of syllables for each line as follows: 5 – 7 – 5 for a total of 17 syllables.

Example: running jumping child
                      flying swooping soaring high
                      imagining flight

This simple haiku poem is about a child who is moving about but in his mind, he is in flight. It is about imagination. Notice the words ending in "ing" (verbals) used together to create a consistent effect. Note also the simplicity of topic – one single idea.

A.   Before writing your haiku poems, follow these exercises.

> **Word association**
>
> On the **first** line, make a list of five <u>action words</u> associated with each of the following ideas.
>
> On the **second** line, write <u>descriptive words</u> of colour, sound, smell, or shape that are associated with the senses for that subject.
>
> On the **third** line, write <u>items</u> that are associated with each topic.

Example:

Swimming

Action:	1. splashing	2. diving	3. floating	4. sinking	5. plunging
Sensory:	1. blue	2. fresh	3. cool	4. deep	5. chilly
Items:	1. towel	2. sand	3. wind	4. waves	5. surf board

Dining out

Action: 1. _____ 2. _____ 3. _____ 4. _____ 5. _____

Sensory: 1. _____ 2. _____ 3. _____ 4. _____ 5. _____

Items: 1. _____ 2. _____ 3. _____ 4. _____ 5. _____

Schoolyard

Action: 1. _____ 2. _____ 3. _____ 4. _____ 5. _____

Sensory: 1. _____ 2. _____ 3. _____ 4. _____ 5. _____

Items: 1. _____ 2. _____ 3. _____ 4. _____ 5. _____

Birthday party

Action: 1. _____ 2. _____ 3. _____ 4. _____ 5. _____

Sensory: 1. _____ 2. _____ 3. _____ 4. _____ 5. _____

Items: 1. _____ 2. _____ 3. _____ 4. _____ 5. _____

Hockey

Action: 1. _____ 2. _____ 3. _____ 4. _____ 5. _____

Sensory: 1. _____ 2. _____ 3. _____ 4. _____ 5. _____

Items: 1. _____ 2. _____ 3. _____ 4. _____ 5. _____

9

Writing Haiku Poems

B. From the lists you created in (A), choose two topics to compose Haiku poems. Create an interesting title for each.

Poem A

_____

_____

_____

_____

Poem B

_____

_____

_____

_____

C. Here is a list of words with the number of syllables in parentheses. Use some of these words in addition to your own to form Haiku poetry.

> Group the words that best suit your topic. For example, if you are composing a poem about night, you may use the following words: midnight, mysterious, scary, sky, lonely, moonlight, stars, clouds, black...

shimmering	(3)	midnight	(2)	scary	(2)
beautiful	(3)	golden	(2)	glow	(1)
mysterious	(4)	whispering	(3)	sad	(1)
		laughing	(2)	bright	(1)
		happiness	(3)	sky	(1)
		happy	(2)	lonely	(2)
		flowing	(2)	castles	(2)

flowers (2)
crash (1)
sand (1)
sunfish (2)
sailboat (2)

sunset (2)
stars (1)
black (1)
bloom (1)
surf (1)
waves (1)
breezes (2)

moonlight (2)
clouds (1)
splash (1)
green (1)

Title

_____

_____

_____

_____

Title

_____

_____

_____

_____

D. **Add words of your own to complete the following haiku poem.**

Title   **Autumn Morning**

First line ➡ _____ ➡ *5 syllables*

red yellow orange and brown ➡ *7 syllables*

Third line ➡ _____ ➡ *5 syllables*

10 Narrative Writing

Narrative writing is to tell a brief story. It is structured in three parts:

(a) Beginning – topic sentence; this is the controlling idea of your story
(b) Middle – the details that support your topic
(c) End – the conclusion to reinforce the controlling idea

The three "Ws" of writing:
1. What – the controlling idea of your story
2. Who – for whom you are writing the story; your audience
3. Why – the purpose for your story; why it is useful to the reader

A. For each broad topic below, create two focused topics that offer different points of view on that topic.

Example: Broad topic: Team sports

Focused topic A: Playing a team sport teaches the importance of working with others.

Focused topic B: The problem with team sports is that you must depend on others to succeed.

Notice how each focused topic takes the writer in a different direction.

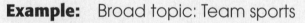

1 **Broad topic: Interesting Summer Holidays**

Focused topic A: _____

Focused topic B: _____

2 **Broad topic: Having a Pet**

Focused topic A: _____

Focused topic B: _____

3 **Broad topic: Preparing for the First Day of School**

Focused topic A: _____

Focused topic B: _____

4 Broad topic: Birthday Celebration

Focused topic A: _____

_____

_____

Focused topic B: _____

_____

5 Broad topic: My Favourite Room in my House

Focused topic A: _____

Focused topic B: _____

6 Broad topic: Relatives Come for a Visit

Focused topic A: _____

Focused topic B: _____

7 Broad topic: Scary Movies

Focused topic A: _____

Focused topic B: _____

8 Broad topic: Making New Friends

Focused topic A: _____

Focused topic B: _____

9 Broad topic: Summer Camp

Focused topic A: _____

Focused topic B: _____

10 Broad topic: Competitive Sports

Focused topic A: _____

Focused topic B: _____

Topic   Topic sentence

 **Writing Narrative Paragraphs**

B.   Use two of the topics above to tell of an incident, a memory, or an event.

PARAGRAPH ONE

Topic: _____

Topic sentence: ◁ *Introduces your focused topic*

_____

Developmental sentences: ◁ *Builds your story from details*

_____

_____

_____

_____

_____

_____

_____

_____

_____

_____

_____

Conclusion: ◁ *Story ending: reason for writing; restates your controlling idea*

_____

_____

_____

Developmental sentences　　　*Conclusion*

PARAGRAPH TWO

Topic: _____

Topic sentence: ◁ *Introduces your focused topic*

_____

Developmental sentences: ◁ *Builds your story from details*

_____

_____

_____

_____

_____

_____

_____

_____

_____

_____

_____

Conclusion: ◁ *Story ending: reason for writing; restates your controlling idea*

_____

_____

_____

11 Vocabulary Development

Root Word Quiz

A. **Use the clue to discover the new word developed from the word given.**

Example:

hair – a design or style – hairdo

1.	stamp	– cattle gone wild – _____
2.	relate	– a cousin or an aunt, for example – _____
3.	try	– happens in a courtroom – _____
4.	camp	– the location of your tent – _____
5.	cycle	– one who rides a bike – _____
6.	attract	– to take away one's attention – _____
7.	collide	– when two vehicles crash – _____
8.	sense	– silliness – _____
9.	capture	– one who gets caught – _____
10.	victor	– how to describe the winner – _____
11.	fix	– encloses the light bulb – _____
12.	pair	– to fix something – _____
13.	incidence	– happen at the same time – _____
14.	collect	– art or stamps, for example – _____
15.	snow	– travels over the snow – _____
16.	coincide	– happen at the same time – _____

17.	nature	– comes from nature – _____
18.	comic	– when it's funny, it's – _____
19.	auto	– works on its own – _____
20.	arrange	– to arrange again or differently – _____

Transitional Words and Conjunctions

Transitional words join short sentences by making one subordinate to the other – that is, one depends on the other for full meaning.

Example: John walked home. His father couldn't pick him up from school.
Because his father couldn't pick him up from school, John walked home.

Conjunctions such as "and", "or", and "but" also join sentences.

Example: John wanted to walk home. His father picked him up from school.
John wanted to walk home **but** his father picked him up from school.

B.   **Join each of the following short sentences with either a transitional word or a conjunction from the word bank below.**

| because | but | when | if | once | although | so |
| as soon as | after | then | while | even though | |

1. Mary called her friend on the telephone. She got no answer.

_____

2. The game was over. Everyone went home.

_____

3. You come over to my house.   We can play computer games.

_____

4.	The storm was over. The sun came out.

_____

5.	He waited for hours for his friends to show up. It started to get dark.

_____

6.	The school bell rang. Summer holidays had started.

_____

7.	He was the team captain. He had to be a leader.

_____

8.	They ate dinner. They had dessert.

_____

_____

9.	His new bike was very fast. It was too big for him.

_____

10.	His alarm went off. He was late for school.

_____

11.	They were the first to arrive. They still waited a long time in line.

_____

_____

12.	They were camping in the mountains. A bear visited their campsite.

_____

_____

C. In each of the following sentences, provide a subordinate clause that suits the meaning of the sentence in the space after the transitional word.

> **Example:**
>
> Although _____it started to rain_____ , they went swimming anyway.

1. After they _____ , they stopped for lunch.

2. Even though the students _____ , they still had trouble finishing the assignment.

3. While they _____ , their friends cheered them on.

4. If she _____ , she will win the trophy.

5. Because he _____ , he stayed home from school.

6. Since he _____ , he has had trouble walking.

D. Add the main clause to each of the sentences below.

1. After they finished eating the whole pie, they _____ _____ .

2. Whenever the sisters go shopping, they always _____ .

3. Because they were best friends, they always _____ .

4. He would have won the game but he _____ .

5. Even though she studied for the test, she _____ .

6. She bought a new dress and she _____ .

7. Either you stay at home tonight or _____ .

8. If there is a large snowfall, we will _____ .

12 Expository Writing

An **expository paragraph** is often written to explain something, to give the reader information, or to persuade the reader about a certain idea.

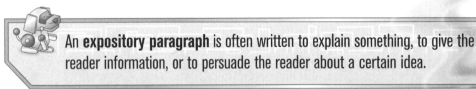

Building a Campfire

Although sitting around a campfire is one of the great joys of camping, building a long lasting, roaring campfire is not a simple task. Often campers simply pile up a few twigs, drop on a couple of logs, stuff in a few rolls of newspaper, and ignite. Unfortunately, they may be disappointed when the fire blazes momentarily, then extinguishes itself just as quickly. The first step in building a campfire is to gather numerous dry twigs and bark shavings and create a pile. Next, add small sticks around your pile in a tepee-like fashion. The tepee shape allows air to get in underneath the pile which the fire needs to maintain a flame. Build the pile by adding larger twigs and sticks; be sure to keep the tepee shape. Find an opening and ignite the dry bark shavings and twigs used as the base of your pile. As the fire builds, add larger pieces of wood. Never simply toss logs on to the pile as it will flatten your tepee shape and no air will

Keep to the writing format of: Topic Sentence + Body Sentences + Conclusion.

get in below the pile. At this point you should be enjoying a roaring fire but be mindful to add wood consistently to maintain enough fuel to keep your fire going.

A. **Identify the following in "Building a Campfire".**

1. Purpose of writing "Building a Campfire": _____

    _____

2. Topic sentence: _____

    _____

3. Concluding sentence: _____

    _____

Summer in the City

When the summer arrives, many people look forward to leaving the city. However, the city offers a variety of interesting ways to spend the hot, lazy days of summer. For those of you who find sitting around a cottage in the middle of the wilderness boring, consider what the city has to offer. When the weather gets unbearably hot, visit one of the many outdoor swimming pools. Or, spend the afternoon in a cool, dark, air-conditioned movie theatre. If you're a cyclist, you can travel the parkland trails that crisscross the city. A visit to the zoo is always interesting, particularly since many newborn animals have arrived in the spring. For the sporting type, there is free tennis at city courts, volleyball at the beach, and skateboarding at a number of specially designed facilities. In fact, you could choose a different activity almost every day. If you should run out of things to do, visit the local mall. There, you can browse record stores, get an ice cream treat, check out the latest computer games, or window shop the latest fashions. Whatever your preference, the city in the summer is a lively place with something for everyone.

B.   Identify the following in "Summer in the City".

1.   Purpose of writing "Summer in the City": _____

_____

2.   Topic sentence: _____

_____

3.   Concluding sentence: _____

_____

Challenge

Provide a concluding sentence of your own for "Summer in the City".

_____

C. **Compose an explanatory paragraph using one of the following topics.**

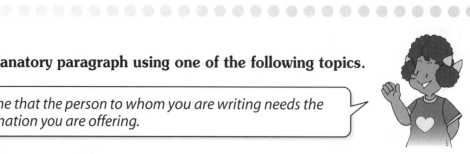

Assume that the person to whom you are writing needs the information you are offering.

The best place to do homework
The best way to learn how to swim
Using the Internet
Making the perfect sandwich
Taking care of a pet

Topic: _____

Topic sentence:

_____

Body sentences:

_____

_____

_____

_____

_____

_____

_____

_____

_____

Concluding sentence:

_____

_____

_____

D. Compose a persuasive paragraph using one of the following topics.

Rollerblading is the best exercise.
Swimming in a pool is better than swimming on a lake.
Schools give too much homework.
Summer holidays are too long.
It's great having an older brother (or sister).

Topic: _____

Topic sentence:

_____

Body sentences:

_____

_____

_____

_____

_____

_____

_____

Concluding sentence:

_____

_____

13 | Le Tour de France

The Tour de France

is the biggest cycling event in the world. In 1902, two men <u>concocted</u> an idea to hold a bicycle race across the French countryside. Beginning in early July each year, the Tour <u>dominates</u> the <u>fascination</u> of the French people for three weeks.

The 2003 Tour de France was particularly significant for two reasons: first, it was the 100th <u>anniversary</u> of the race; second, Lance Armstrong, the world's greatest cyclist, was attempting to win his fifth <u>consecutive</u> race, a <u>feat</u> accomplished only once before in the history of the Tour. On July 5, 2003, 198 cyclists began the 3,427.5-kilometre race through the French countryside. They would ride for 22 days through 20 stages, including 7 mountain stages, <u>culminating</u> in Paris. On July 27, only one rider would be wearing the yellow jersey <u>signifying</u> victory.

The accomplishments of the cyclists during the Tour are <u>indicated</u> by coloured jerseys. The yellow jersey is worn by the winner of a stage in the race. The green is for the fastest sprinter in a given stage. The polka-dot jersey, the climber's jersey, is won by accumulating bonus points during the mountain climbing stages. The white jersey is <u>reserved</u> for the best young rider. Each day <u>anxious</u> spectators who line the country roads of <u>rural</u> France wait to see who is wearing which jersey. For a rider, wearing a <u>designated</u> jersey for any part of the race is a great <u>honour</u>. To win the Tour, however, a rider does not necessarily have to win one of the stages. Twice in the history of the Tour, riders have had the best overall time without winning a single stage. Each stage is timed <u>individually</u> and the rider with the shortest <u>accumulated</u> time wins the race.

<u>Undeniably</u> the story of the 2003 Tour was Lance Armstrong's quest for a fifth consecutive victory. Armstrong, who had <u>overcome</u> cancer to return to racing, is <u>admired</u> by the world for his courage, <u>endurance</u>, and <u>determination</u>. Renowned for his superior mountain climbing ability, Armstrong battled the mountainous <u>terrain</u> and the gruelling July heat to <u>record</u> his fifth consecutive victory. He defeated Jan Ullrich of Germany by a margin of only one minute and one second – <u>remarkably</u> close after 21 days of racing.

But for Lance Armstrong, the <u>quest</u> is not yet complete. He will now train <u>vigorously</u> in <u>relentless</u> <u>pursuit</u> of one goal – to become the only cyclist to win the Tour de France six consecutive times. The world waits in <u>anticipation</u> for July, 2004 when once again the greatest cyclists in the world will assemble in Paris with one thing in mind – defeat Lance Armstrong.

Words in Context

Read the passage and match each underlined word with a meaning from the list according to the "context" of the sentence in which it appears. Place the letter of the appropriate meaning beside the word.

Paragraph One

1. concocted _____   2. dominates _____   3. fascination _____

A. takes control of, rules over, governs, commands
B. came up with, devised, planned, created
C. allure, power of attraction, excitement

Use the word "dominates" in a sentence to show its meaning.

_____

Paragraph Two

1. anniversary _____
2. consecutive _____
3. feat _____
4. culminating _____
5. signifying _____

A. representing an idea, showing, proving, illustrating
B. occurs every year, annual
C. accomplishment, achievement
D. ending, finishing, completing
E. occurs one after the other, in a row

Use the word "consecutive" in a sentence to show its meaning.

_____

Paragraph Three

1. indicated _____
2. reserved _____
3. anxious _____
4. rural _____
5. designated _____
6. honour _____
7. individually _____
8. accumulated _____

A. out of the city, non-urban, countryside area
B. built up, added on to, totalling
C. in anticipation of, eager, nervous, impatient
D. signified, pointed to, shown
E. limited to, held for, accounted for
F. credit, award, recognition
G. made for, matched up, appointed
H. for one person only, for each person

Use the word "accumulated" in a sentence to show its meaning.

_____

Paragraph Four

1. undeniably ____
2. overcome ____
3. admired ____
4. endurance ____
5. determination ____
6. terrain ____
7. record ____
8. remarkably ____

A. physical strength, power to withstand, longevity, long lasting
B. noticeably, strangely, oddly, surprisingly
C. without question, no doubt
D. valued, regarded, honoured, loved
E. make a note of, enter as fact, mark, indicate, register
F. will-power, devotion, be firm, a decision made
G. land, countryside, geographical area, region
H. defeated, ruled over, endured, survived, struggled through

Use the word "remarkably" in a sentence of your own showing its meaning.

_____

Paragraph Five

1. quest ____
2. vigorously ____
3. relentless ____
4. pursuit ____
5. anticipation ____

A. waiting for, keen to see happen, excited for something to come
B. goal, pursuit, attempt, search for
C. highly physical, maximum physical effort, lively, brisk, energetic
D. without stopping, determined, unending
E. search for, seek, desire to achieve, chase for

Use the word "vigorously" in a sentence of your own showing its meaning.

_____

14 Informal Writing

Informal writing does not always follow precise rules of grammar. The sentence structure of informal writing is often quite casual. People write informally in emails, notes, friendly letters, invitations, thank you notes, or on greeting cards.

A.   Rewrite the following postcard note to make it informal.

Dear Dana,

Today we arrived in Dublin and my cousins came to meet us at the airport. I'm really excited about meeting all our relatives. Tomorrow we will travel to Cork City, and later on, we will tour the Ring of Kerry. Ireland is beautiful; the scenery is breath taking.

We have only been here a few hours but I think I'm already developing an Irish accent. My cousins think that I speak with a Canadian accent – whatever that is. For the third week of this holiday, we will be visiting more relatives in London. I hope all is well with you. I will write again soon.

Sincerely,
Lauren

Dana Shank

123 Popular Street

Toronto, Ontario

C2W V3X

Dana Shank

123 Popular Street

Toronto, Ontario

C2W V3X

The Utterance

An utterance is an incomplete sentence that offers a complete thought. Utterances are acceptable in dialogue and informal writing.

Example: Do you want a ride home? No, thanks.

"No, thanks" is an utterance because it does not have a subject or a verb but it offers a complete thought.

Informal writing with brief sentences or utterances is particularly useful when you have limited space such as in notes or postcards.

B.   Assume you are on holiday in a place you've dreamt of visiting. Write a postcard to a friend or family member giving as many details as possible in a small space.

14

C. Compose an invitation to a birthday party. Include all the necessary details such as date, time, place, and any other details. Use a large, bold title to announce the event.

Want Ads

Newspapers often charge by the words for advertisements. To save space, complete sentences are not used. Note that the ad below gives details about the product and it also adds the statement "great deal" to try to entice the buyer.

10-speed Road Racer for Sale

Boy's 10-speed road racer. Red with white detailing. New tires, include lock. Excellent shape. Great deal. Asking $75.00.

D. Assume that you are trying to sell something. Write ads for two of the following products:

a.	your desktop computer	b.	your disc player
c.	your skis	d.	a puppy from the new litter
e.	a computer game	f.	your old skateboard
g.	a doll collection	h.	music CDs

1.

2.

Synonyms – Facts about Canada

In each of the following paragraphs, the words in bold can be replaced by synonyms numbered below. Place the number of the replacement synonym beside the word in bold.

The History of Canadian Flags

The first Canadian flag was likely the St. George's Cross, a fifteenth century English flag. John Cabot reached the east coast of Canada in 1497 and erected the flag claiming the land for England. In 1534, Jacques Cartier **hoisted** ◯ the fleur-de-lis firmly **establishing** ◯ French **sovereignty** ◯ in Canada. In the early 1760's, Canada was **ceded** ◯ to the United Kingdom and the Royal Union flag, more commonly known as the Union Jack, became the **official** ◯ flag of Canada.

1 setting up

2 raised

3 rule

4 surrendered

5 standard

The Red Ensign flag, a cross between the Union Jack and a shield bearing the arms of Nova Scotia, Ontario, New Brunswick, and Quebec, **originated** ◯ as a Merchant Marine flag in 1707. Never **officially** ◯ **acknowledged** ◯ as the flag of Canada on land, the British admiralty accepted the Red Ensign as the official Canadian **maritime** ◯ flag. In 1924, the Order of Council changed the unofficial Red Ensign replacing the **original** ◯ shield with the Canadian Coat of Arms. A government order in 1945 **declared** ◯ this new

version ◯ to be the interim flag of Canada until a new one was **designed** ◯.

In 1965, the Canadian Ensign was replaced by the current red and white maple

leaf flag that is the proud **symbol** ◯ of Canada.

6	nautical or marine	7	began	8	accepted
9	announced	10	formally	11	type
12	representation	13	first	14	created

Nunavut
Canada's New Territory

Nunavut, Canada's newest **territory** ◯, gets its name

from the Inuktitut word meaning "our land". Nunavut officially became a territory

on April 1, 1999. This vast region **extends** ◯ northwest from Hudson Bay beyond

the tree line to the North Pole. In all, Nunavut's **expanse** ◯ is an **astounding** ◯

2,000,000 square kilometres.

The Nunavut landscape is **remarkably** ◯ **diverse** ◯. The North Baffin

region is a mixture of mountain ranges and fiords while the Kivalliq area is flat.

15	stretches	16	surprisingly	17	shocking
18	region	19	vastness	20	assorted

Nunavut's population is the youngest in Canada – its median age is only 22

years. The population is growing rapidly with an **impressive** ◯ 10% increase

since its **inception** ◯ in 1999. Most of the Nunavut population is made up of the

Inuit people. There are 26 communities in Nunavut including its capital, Iqaluit, which has a population of close to 6,000. Many Nunavut communities are not **accessible** ( ) by road or rail. Basic needs including food and fuel must be **transported** ( ) by plane. Consequently, goods are very expensive. Most citizens of Nunavut are **employed** ( ) by the three levels of government: municipal, federal, and territorial. As new industries develop, particularly in the mining **sector** ( ) , more job **opportunities** ( ) will **emerge** ( ) . There is also growth in fisheries and tourism, and there is a growing interest in Inuit art, **particularly** ( ) stone carvings and prints.

21 hired	**22** division or section	**23** appear
24 beginning	**25** extraordinary	**26** approachable
27 sent	**28** chances	**29** especially

The people of Nunavut speak four languages (French, English, Inuinaqtun, and Inuktitut), live in an area that is one-fifth the size of Canada, and have an extremely low population **density** ( ) . It is a challenge for the federal government to meet the **unique** ( ) needs of the region. **Primary** ( ) concerns for the government of Canada in this region are health, education, and job creation. Although Nunavut presents **unprecedented** ( ) challenges, the people of Nunavut remain **optimistic** ( ) .

| **30** first | **31** thickness | **32** different or special |
| **33** new | **34** confident |

The Canadian National Anthem — "O Canada"

The Official Lyrics of "O Canada"

O Canada!
Our home and native land!
True patriot love in all thy sons command.

With glowing hearts we see thee rise,
The True North strong and free!

From far and wide,
O Canada, we stand on guard for thee.

God keep our land glorious and free!
O Canada, we stand on guard for thee.

O Canada, we stand on guard for thee.

Our national anthem, as we know it today, became the official anthem on July 1, 1980. However, the **initial** ( ) singing of this song took place 100 years **prior** ( ). Calixa Lavallée, a renowned **composer** ( ) of his time, is credited with composing the music to **accompany** ( ) the French lyrics written by Sir Adolphe-Basil Routhier. Over the years there have been **numerous** ( ) English **renditions** ( ) of the song but the lyrics of Robert Stanley Weir, written in 1908, became the official English version. This version remained **unaltered** ( ) until 1968 when the Canadian government made **minor** ( ) changes. The French version has remained unchanged.

35	unchanged	36	small	37	first
		38	many	39	before
40	versions	41	song-writer	42	go along with

A. Use the context of each of the sentences below to determine the meaning of the italicized word. Circle the <u>best</u> synonym from the list provided.

1. The table was *situated* in the centre of the room.

   located   placed   found   left

2. The *boundary* of the playing field was fenced.

   place   limitations   area   situation

3. They set up camp at the *base* of the mountain.

   apex   centre   edge   bottom

4. The time was *approximately* four o'clock.

   nearly   always   forever   exactly

5. The room was *accessible* by a door off the hall.

   barred   available   cut off   approachable

6. His dog will *venture* into the street if not leashed.

   slip   wander   fall   cross

7. For *traction* he wore spiked shoes.

   speed   grip   style   efficiency

8. He *accumulated* all his money from working many jobs.

   gathered   collected   earned   found

9. The melting of the ice was *gradual* in the morning sun.

   sudden   abrupt   slow   wet

10. The cell was only *detectable* through a microscope.

    known   accessible   visible   shown

11. They will *establish* an award table near the track and field events.

    organize   set up   build   create

12. The rain and wind of the unusually *harsh* weather stopped the play-day.

    difficult   rough   balmy   rugged

228   Complete EnglishSmart • **Grade 5**

13. He was concerned for the *environment* particularly the preservation of forests.

   surroundings   location   place   neighbourhood

14. The *conservation* of wildlife in their natural habitat is important.

   survival   protection   neglect   concern

15. The rules of the game were *enforced* by the referee.

   applied   altered   declined   forgotten

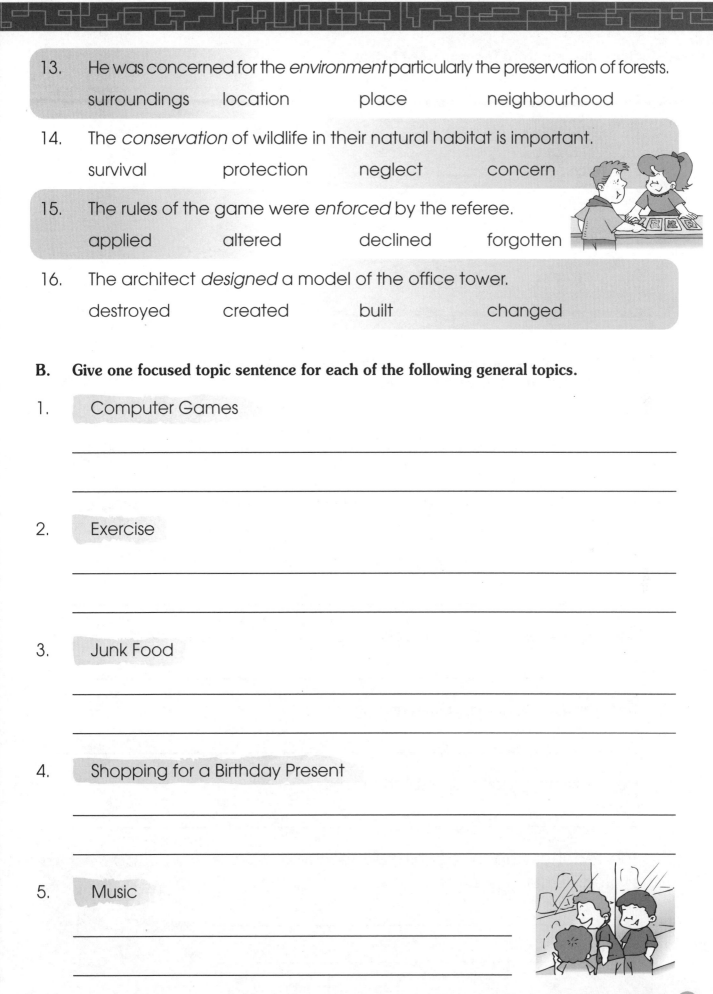

16. The architect *designed* a model of the office tower.

   destroyed   created   built   changed

B. Give one focused topic sentence for each of the following general topics.

1. Computer Games

   _____

   _____

2. Exercise

   _____

   _____

3. Junk Food

   _____

   _____

4. Shopping for a Birthday Present

   _____

   _____

5. Music

   _____

   _____

C. State the root word for each word below.

1. statement _____

2. coincidence _____

3. relationship _____

4. attraction _____

5. captive _____

6. collision _____

7. sensibility _____

8. incidentally _____

9. victorious _____

10. repairing _____

D. Join the following pairs of sentences with either a conjunction or a transitional adverb from the list below.

Use each conjunction only once.

as soon as   although   while   and   because

1. He walked home. He missed the school bus.

_____

2. She invited her friends over for a sleepover. They ordered pizza.

_____

3. The game continued. It was raining.

_____

4. He cooked hot dogs. She set the table.

_____

5. The teacher began teaching. The students were seated at their desks.

_____

_____

E. **Match the italicized words with their meanings. A brief phrase is given to add context to each of the italicized words.**

Group A

1. *concoct* an idea
2. *dominate* the race
3. *fascination* of the fans
4. 100th *anniversary*
5. *consecutive* victories
6. *culminating* at the finish line
7. *signifying* the winner
8. an amazing *feat* of strength
9. *reserved* for the winner
10. from city to *rural* area

A ending
B countryside
C yearly celebration
D accomplishment
E awe, surprise
F saved
G many in a row
H indicating
I come up with, develop
J control, take over

Group B

1. *individual* time trial
2. *accumulated* time
3. *overcome* difficulty
4. *admired* by everyone
5. *endurance* to continue the race
6. *determination* to succeed
7. mountain *terrain*
8. training *vigorously*
9. *pursuit* of victory
10. *anticipation* of the beginning of the race

A get over, solve
B strength, ability
C landscape, country
D expecting, expectation
E total of, added up
F strenuously, with great effort
G for one person
H quest for, search for
I loved
J desire

F.   **Match each of the words on the left with its synonym.**

1.   hoisted

2.   establishing

3.   impressive

4.   diverse

5.   optimistic

6.   declared

7.   version

8.   maritime

9.   inception

10. accessible

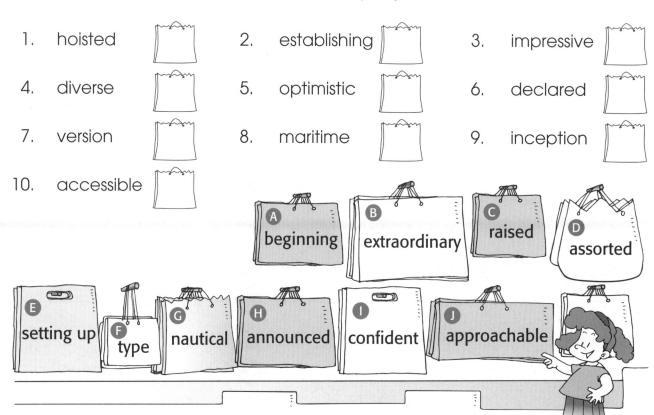

A beginning

B extraordinary

C raised

D assorted

E setting up

F type

G nautical

H announced

I confident

J approachable

G.   **Re-write each of the following sentences, using a more descriptive synonym or phrase to replace the underlined word.**

1.   The <u>house</u> is the biggest in the neighbourhood.

_____

2.   Uncle Jeff's <u>car</u> ran on both gasoline and electricity.

_____

3.   We were <u>happy</u> that our team finally won.

_____

4.   We could hardly stand the <u>loud</u> music.

_____

5.   Everyone enjoyed the <u>good</u> show.

_____

H. Compose an expository paragraph on the following topic.

Topic: The Best Time of the Year

Topic Sentence:

_____

_____

Body Sentences:

_____

_____

_____

_____

_____

_____

_____

_____

Concluding Sentence:

_____

_____

_____

Welcome

Language Games

Look at the pictures. Complete the Sports Crossword Puzzle.

SPORTS
Crossword Puzzle

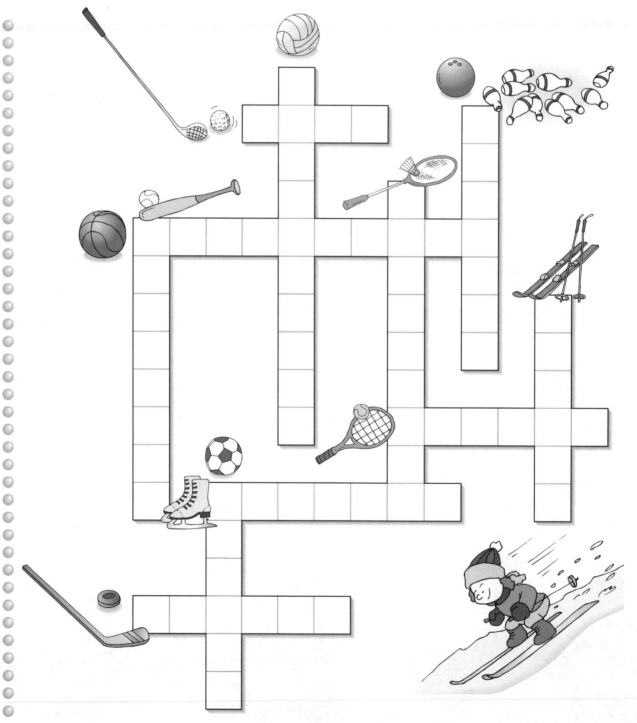

Complete the word slides to turn "main" into "trap". Change only one letter for each slide.

m a i n

⬇

☐ a i n

⬇

☐ ☐ ☐ ☐

⬇

g ☐ i n

⬇

☐ ☐ ☐ ☐

⬇

☐ r i p

⬇

☐ ☐ ☐ ☐

3 Complete the crossword puzzle with synonyms of the clue words.

Across	Down
A. opportunity	1. afraid
B. clue	2. watchful
C. precise	3. use
D. fix	4. enormous
E. hop	5. fly
F. genuine	6. stop
	7. hide

Synonym Crossword Puzzle

4

Fill in the missing letters to complete the words.

1.

	I	S	
A			I
R	1		L
	T	I	L

2.

	I	N	G
I			A
C	2		T
	I	T	

3.

P	E	E	
O			I
R	3		V
	A	K	

4.

	A	I	
O			E
P	4		A
	V	E	R

5.

T	H	A	
A			I
I	5		C
	O	O	

6.

	I	L	
A			A
K	6		R
	A	R	N

Find out what the monsters say by unscrambling the letters.

EW VILE NO A ELAPTN
ARF YAAW OFMR TAHER.
EW ATWN OT KEAM
WNE NIRFSED. NAC EW
EB ESRFIDN?

_____

_____

_____

_____

6

Complete the crossword puzzle with antonyms of the clue words.

Antonym Crossword Puzzle

Across

A. coarse
B. relaxed
C. shrink
D. bright
E. inching
F. accept

Down

1. favourable
2. rare
3. celebrate
4. bland
5. daring
6. miserable

1. A N T O N Y M S

7 Complete the word slides to turn "reap" into "well". Change only one letter for each slide.

r | e | a | p

□ | e | a | p

□ | □ | □ | □

h | e | a | □

□ | □ | □ | □

s | e | □ | l

□ | □ | □ | □

8 Circle twelve insects in the Insect Word Search.

h	c	d	l	f	j	a	n	e	m	g	a	e
f	r	m	g	w	w	h	q	b	a	n	h	b
c	i	c	a	d	a	c	n	s	n	e	j	l
d	c	h	m	o	s	q	u	i	t	o	c	a
m	k	b	o	b	p	e	p	d	i	g	o	d
k	e	p	f	l	b	i	l	g	s	l	c	y
r	t	l	d	j	e	n	f	a	j	c	k	b
c	a	o	v	c	e	u	r	o	t	p	r	u
h	f	c	l	p	t	z	x	i	v	b	o	g
d	b	u	m	b	l	e	b	e	e	i	a	c
a	k	s	e	f	e	i	y	a	m	q	c	i
j	m	t	d	o	q	l	r	m	o	t	h	m
k	a	n	a	n	t	x	b	c	s	r	o	g

Insect Word Search

9

Complete the crossword puzzle with homophones of the clue words.

Homophone Crossword Puzzle

H O M O P H O N E S

Across

A. wait
B. waist
C. rose
D. pair
E. not

Down

1. which
2. face
3. eight
4. bear
5. plane
6. sail
7. wail

10 Match the pictures to form compound words. Write the words on the lines.

1    

2    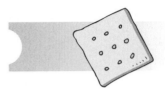

3    

4    

5    

6   

1. _____   2. _____

3. _____   4. _____

5. _____   6. _____

11

Circle twelve stationery items in the Stationery Word Search.

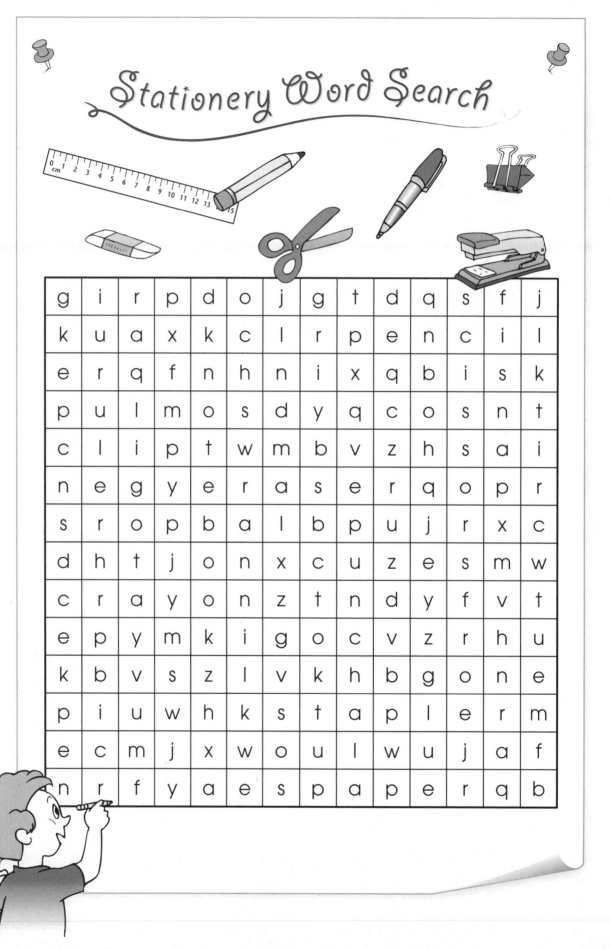

Stationery Word Search

g	i	r	p	d	o	j	g	t	d	q	s	f	j
k	u	a	x	k	c	l	r	p	e	n	c	i	l
e	r	q	f	n	h	n	i	x	q	b	i	s	k
p	u	l	m	o	s	d	y	q	c	o	s	n	t
c	l	i	p	t	w	m	b	v	z	h	s	a	i
n	e	g	y	e	r	a	s	e	r	q	o	p	r
s	r	o	p	b	a	l	b	p	u	j	r	x	c
d	h	t	j	o	n	x	c	u	z	e	s	m	w
c	r	a	y	o	n	z	t	n	d	y	f	v	t
e	p	y	m	k	i	g	o	c	v	z	r	h	u
k	b	v	s	z	l	v	k	h	b	g	o	n	e
p	i	u	w	h	k	s	t	a	p	l	e	r	m
e	c	m	j	x	w	o	u	l	w	u	j	a	f
n	r	f	y	a	e	s	p	a	p	e	r	q	b

12

Complete the crossword puzzle with synonyms of the clue words.

Across

A. defeat
B. stiff
C. damaging
D. grow
E. chilly
F. delicate
G. broad

Down

1. strange
2. quick
3. friendly
4. competent
5. slender
6. fortunate
7. hard

S Y N O N Y M S

large = big

13 Complete the word slides to turn "fast" into "kite". Change only one letter for each slide.

fast

☐ a s t

☐ ☐ ☐ ☐

m ☐ s s

☐ ☐ ☐ ☐

m i ☐ t

☐ ☐ ☐ ☐

☐ i t e

14 Colour the correct box in each column to find out what Paula the Polar Bear says.

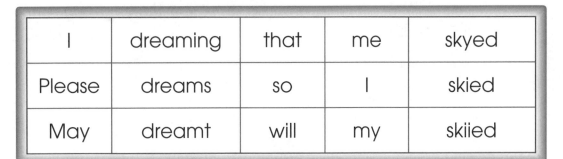

I	dreaming	that	me	skyed
Please	dreams	so	I	skied
May	dreamt	will	my	skiied

by	Santa Clause	in	night	?
up	Santa Claus	the	day	,
with	Santer Claus	last	thing	.

15

Complete the crossword puzzle with antonyms of the clue words.

Across

- A. easy
- B. shout
- C. arrive
- D. guilty
- E. decline
- F. relaxing

Antonym Crossword Puzzle

A N T O N Y M S

Down

1. split
2. praise
3. common
4. clear
5. blunt
6. pessimistic

16 Circle ten "Halloween" words in the Holloween Word Search.

Halloween
Word Search

l	n	p	h	d	i	b	g	r	q	y	p	e	n
x	f	H	m	a	e	z	s	w	o	l	u	h	o
c	t	a	n	m	c	H	a	m	h	z	m	j	c
o	b	k	j	y	p	l	n	x	w	i	p	u	g
s	h	d	g	m	o	j	t	r	i	c	k	g	t
t	k	a	w	h	e	q	r	e	l	q	i	H	a
u	H	a	l	l	o	w	e	e	n	t	n	m	k
m	d	f	z	t	p	s	a	y	i	p	q	w	f
e	o	h	t	l	c	n	t	w	s	b	a	e	j
s	p	i	d	e	r	h	s	g	i	a	c	x	o
b	f	n	y	q	s	k	e	l	e	t	o	n	m
p	j	f	x	l	b	z	k	x	d	s	c	p	r
d	z	w	a	r	c	i	g	b	r	f	z	h	l
m	l	x	i	q	j	n	p	o	m	k	y	m	k

1 Cats

A.
1. 60 million
2. Miacis
3. 35 million
4. 12,000
5. big and small
6. cheetah
7. small cat
8. hunters
9. 41
10. cheetah

B.
1. (students) ; Ottawa ; (car)
2. Smith ; Maple Road Public School ; (years)
3. (tourists) ; Japan ; Niagara Falls ; Maid of the Mist ; (ride)
4. (boys) ; (soccer) ; (girls) ; (baseball)
5. Jenny ; (friend) ; Susan ; (play) ; A Christmas Story
6. (puddle) ; (step)
7. CN Tower ; (structures) ; North America
8. Jones ; England ; Buckingham Palace

C.
1. famous
2. unsuspecting
3. classification
4. extinct
5. distinct
6. broad
7. powerful
8. developed
9. domestic
10. methods
11. stalk
12. popular

2 The "Horseless Carriage" (1)

A.
1. O   2. F   3. F   4. F
5. O   6. F   7. O   8. F
9. O   10. F   11. F   12. F

B. (Answers will vary.)

C.
1. N   2. A   3. A   4. A
5. A   6. N   7. N   8. A
9. A   10. A

D. (Answers will vary.)

E.
1. inspired
2. capable
3. paved
4. critics
5. invention
6. imagine
7. development
8. perfected
9. bicycle
10. improvement
11. successful
12. powered
13. suburbs
14. mechanics

3 The "Horseless Carriage" (2)

A.
1. Assembly line production was introduced.
2. Ford used the assembly line method.
3. More cars were produced.
4. Ford paid his workers $5 a day.
5. Buyers wanted the latest model.
6. The "payment plan" was introduced.

B.
1. T ; lined ; (the parade route)
2. T ; watched ; (the parade)
3. T ; wore ; (bright costumes)
4. I ; played
5. T ; handed ; (candy)
6. I ; smiled
7. I ; lasted
8. I ; stayed
9. T ; tossed ; (fiery torches)
10. T ; filled ; (the sky)
11. I ; smiled
12. I ; started ; ended

C.

4 Influenza – More Than Just a Cold

A.
1. flu
2. fever
3. appetite
4. pneumonia
5. 25
6. 5
7. Antibiotics
8. vaccines
9. CDC
10. shots
11. elderly
12. illnesses

B. (Suggested answers)
1. The biggest problem the medical community faces today is that flu strains are constantly changing.
2. The elderly and people with chronic illnesses are the most at risk because they are often too weak to fight off the disease.

C.
1. They
2. He
3. We
4. She

D.
1. me ; Indirect
2. him ; Direct
3. her ; Indirect
4. him ; Indirect
5. him ; Direct

E.
1. accept
2. adept
3. edition
4. berth
5. council
6. Lay
7. minor
8. role
9. stationery ; stationary
10. altar

5   Treasures of the Orient (1)

A.
1. T   2. F   3. F   4. T
5. F   6. T   7. F   8. F
9. T   10. T   11. F   12. F
13. T

B. (Suggested answers)
1. They were looking for a quicker and less difficult trade route. The land route was mountainous and time-consuming.
2. The Europeans could offer manufactured goods for trade in the Orient.

C.
1. their   2. his ; his
3. our   4. your
5. her   6. mine

D.
1. who   2. which
3. that   4. whom

E.

COLUMN A	COLUMN B
channelled	cost
established	to ask for
expense	sent in a direction
excursion	heritage or nationality
objective	joined again
marketable	encouraged
request	made, developed
culture	trip
reunited	purpose
inspired	easy to sell

F. (Answers will vary.)

6   Treasures of the Orient (2)

A. (Suggested answers)
1. Europeans thought that trade with the Orient would be profitable because they would be selling goods that Europeans could not otherwise obtain such as silk and spices.
2. The route around Africa was already of interest to many countries. Those who believed that the world was round thought that an alternate and perhaps safer and quicker route might be found by sailing west.
3. There were great riches in the Americas. Also it was the discovery of an entire continent that could be claimed by Spain and later settled.
4. Yes. John Cabot discovered the Grand Banks that even today stands as one of the richest fishing areas in the world.
5. Magellan officially completed the journey to the Pacific Ocean, thereby completing the route east to the Orient.
6. One could build an argument for the equal importance of both but the fact that the Americas were discovered and later settled becoming the North and South Americas of today was of monumental significance.
7. Magellan is credited with sailing around the world, confirming the fact that the world is a globe. However, Columbus was the one who initiated the route east, discovering the Americas and paving the way for the expansion of Europe to the Americas.

B.
1. D   2. D   3. I   4. I
5. D   6. D   7. I   8. I

C.
1. Michael   2. bicycle
3. hill   4. he
5. top   6. drink
7. it   8. trip
9. he   10. way
11. bottom

D.
1. routes   2. dispute
3. profit   4. exotic
5. voyage

E. (Answers will vary.)

7   Gypsies – an Endangered Culture

A. (Suggested answers)
Paragraph One:
The Gypsies are one of the many cultural groups that face extinction.
Paragraph Two:
Gypsies are a nomadic culture that make a living by doing many different types of work.
Paragraph Three:
The Eastern European Gypsies had a different lifestyle than those in Western Europe.
Paragraph Four:
Gypsies have assimilated with many other cultures but in many countries they are neither trusted nor welcome.

B. (Suggested answers)
1. Some people do not like the Gypsies because they are thought of as dishonest traders.
2. Many Gypsies have chosen to assimilate with the culture of the country that they inhabit and in doing so, they give up their own cultural characteristics.
3. The Gypsies were considered colourful people because they wore bright, colourful clothing.

C.
1. long ; (slowly)
2. happy ; (enthusiastically) ; Christmas
3. school ; (quietly)
4. loud
5. rock ; (loudly) ; devoted

D. (Answers will vary.)

E. 1. spacious   2. (an) expensive
    3. stormy   4. thrilled
    5. scampered   6. delicious
    7. visited
F. 1. stormy   2. howled
    3. tightly   4. terrified
    5. flashed   6. booming
    7. poured   8. abandoned
    9. patiently   10. subside
   11. gleamed   12. skipped
   13. arrived   14. drenched
   15. steaming

8 The Amazing Helen Keller (1)

A. 1. B   2. C   3. A   4. A
    5. B   6. C
B. 1. girls | played   2. dogs | are
    3. Morning | is   4. wind | howled
    5. holidays | will be
C. 1. Getting school on time ; was
    2. team ; arrived   3. waves ; crashed
    4. Happiness ; is   5. athletes ; are
D. (Free answers)
E. (Suggested answers)
    1. smiled   2. whistled
    3. protected   4. waved
    5. laughed

9 The Amazing Helen Keller (2)

A. 1. The day that Helen ... point in her life.
    2. Helen Keller completed ... seven in all.
    3. This play was turned ... in 1962.
    4. She was determined ... Commission for the Blind.
    5. Anne, who was ... using this method.
    6. At the age of twenty ... four years later.
    7. Remarkably, she specialized ... and philosophy.
    8. She toured England ... of the handicapped.
B. 1. The children bought the candy at the store.
    2. The racing cars roared around the track.
    3. Be careful of slipping on the ice.
    4. The hungry boy ate the steaming hot pizza.
    5. The colourful sailboat drifted across the calm water.
C. 1. appropriate   2. kind
    3. spell   4. able / ability
    5. firm   6. complete
D. 1. helpful   2. impossible
    3. lovable   4. inform / formation
    5. unafraid   6. nervous
    7. movable   8. unclear
    9. disagree / agreeable

10. disprove / improve / provable
11. truthful   12. famous
13. increase   14. intend

Progress Test 1

A. 1. C   2. D   3. B   4. B
    5. A   6. C   7. B   8. B
    9. C   10. A   11. C   12. C
   13. B   14. B   15. B   16. C
   17. C   18. A   19. A   20. C
B. 1. S   2. I   3. D   4. D
    5. D   6. S   7. D
C. 1. his   2. It
    3. We   4. us ; our
    5. their
D. 1. cat | chased   2. moon | shone
    3. Happiness | is   4. students | cheered
    5. He | falls
E. 1. ball   2. gas
    3. fly   4. flowers
    5. shoulders   6. line
F. cold ; windy ; winter ; frozen ; (dangerously) ; slippery ;
    delivery ; (slowly) ; icy ; (cautiously) ; grocery ; (gently) ;
    car ; (tightly) ; (cleverly) ; first
G. 1. He waited inside the shelter for the rain to stop.
    2. Hockey and soccer were his favourite sports.
    3. She joined the skating club when she was just five years old.
    4. The sky was blue and the water was calm.
    5. Awards were given out on the last day of school.
H. 1. broad   2. extinct
    3. stalk   4. exotic
    5. critical   6. domestic
    7. excursion   8. objective
    9. inspired   10. unsuspecting
I. 1. enormous   2. attractive
    3. agreeable   4. swift
    5. extensive   6. towering
    7. hazardous   8. fluffy
    9. firm   10. exit / depart
   11. exit / depart   12. stroll
   13. scurried   14. strike
J. (Answers will vary.)

10 **Who Is the Greatest Hockey Player of All Time?**

A. 1a. Wayne Gretzky
1b. Gordie Howe
2. Orr made end-to-end rushes with the puck.
3a. the MVP
3b. the leading point scorer
3c. the best defenseman
3d. the play-off MVP
4. He had serious knee problems.
5. He was named the tournament MVP.
6. He was a rushing defenseman who was high scoring.

B. (Answers will vary.)

C. 1. (In) ; Adv.   2. (At) ; Adv.
3. (of) ; Adj.   4. (in) ; Adj.
5. (in) ; Adv.   6. (At) ; Adv.
7. (under) ; Adv.   8. (among) ; Adv.
9. (without) ; Adv.   10. (On) ; Adv.

D. 1. given   2. decision
3. fortunate   4. lovely
5. creative   6. carelessness
7. tightened   8. multiplication ; division
9. useful   10. helpful

E. (Any order)
scoring / scorer ; traditionally ; occasionally ; believe ; distinguishing ; milestones ; himself ; furiously ; speculation ; operations ; successful ; exciting

11 **Bicycles, Then and Now**

A.

COLUMN A	COLUMN B
safety bicycle	home of Michaux
modern bicycle	resembled a tricycle
international race	safety bicycle was designed
Paris	ratio of gears
velocipede	first real bicycles appeared
1887	reason for today's use
32 teeth	shifts the chain
8 teeth	units sold per year
4 to 1	Tour de France
environmental concerns	front chainwheel
derailer	smaller front wheel
500	fast, durable, comfortable
19th century	rear chainwheel

B. (Answers will vary.)

C. 1. (Whenever I run too fast)
2. (After we played the game)
3. (because it was an emergency)
4. (as long as he wanted)

5. (Even if they tried harder)
6. (as the sun set)
7. (as if no one could see what he was doing)
8. (Although the students were well-behaved)
9. (while she waited for her friend to call)
10. (that even if he tried, he could not forget what happened)
11. (where he has gone for lunch)
12. (since I wasn't there)
13. (before I could take a photo of it)

D. 1. FAMOUS   2. SAFETY
3. PROPULSION   4. UNITS
5. DIFFERENT   6. RENEWED
7. ROTATIONS   8. COMFORTABLE
9. LEVELS   10. DURABLE

12 **Marilyn Bell – Marathon Swimmer (1)**

A. 1. O   2. F   3. F   4. F
5. F   6. F   7. O   8. F
9. F   10. O   11. O   12. F

B. (Answers will vary.)
C. (Answers will vary.)
D. (Answers will vary.)

13 **Marilyn Bell – Marathon Swimmer (2)**

A. 1. T   2. F   3. T   4. T
5. F   6. F   7. F   8. T
9. T   10. F   11. T   12. T

B. (Answers will vary.)

C. 1. The injured man called for Dr. Smith to come to his aid.
2. Before their trip to London, England, Mr. and Mrs. Anderson called the Department of Immigration to get their documents.
3. The Earl of Sandwich became famous for his invention of the sandwich.
4. Lisa Moore attended the University of Toronto and received a degree in English.
5. She asked, "What time will Professor Higgins give his speech about Pioneers of the Wild West?"
6. Although they were both Canadians, James came from the West and Joan came from the East, so they decided to meet in Winnipeg.
7. The Japanese family arrived in New York on American Airlines and stayed at the Hilton Hotel in upper Manhattan.
8. The Mona Lisa is one of da Vinci's most famous paintings.

D. (Answers will vary.)
E. (Answers will vary.)

14 Meat-Eating Plants

A. 1. carnivorous 2. insects
    3. diet 4. Venus Flytrap
    5. Sticky Sundew 6. nectar
    7. confused 8. enzymes
    9. weeks 10. wind
    11. exoskeleton

B. (Answers will vary.)

C. 1. When Susan went shopping at the local store, she bought milk, bread, cheese, eggs, and butter.
    2. Why do certain sports such as hockey, golf, and tennis cost so much to play?
    3. "Get out of bed right now or you'll be late for school!" my mother yelled. "Don't you realize it's September 5, the first day of school?"
    4. Where would a person go to find good weather, interesting shopping, friendly people, and inexpensive accommodations?
    5. Look out, the tree branch is breaking off!
    6. Hand in your test papers, your special pencils, and your question sheets now.
    7. John's father, Mr. Williams, carried the balls, the bases, and the bats.

D.

Synonym	Word from the reading passage
addition	carnivorous
lands	prey
leak	devoured
victim	nectar
dazed	supplement
food	secrete
decorations	predator
taken in	alights
hunter	dietary
strange	confused
sweet liquid	adornments
meat-eating	absorbed
eaten	unusual

E. (Answers will vary.)

15 Pirates of the Caribbean (1)

A. 1. b 2. a 3. b 4. b
    5. a 6. b

B. 1. The music teacher gave the girls free time to finish the songs.
    2. The lively tune was composed by the girls.
    3. The pizza was made by Sam and Pam.
    4. The whole family enjoyed the pizza.
    5. The car was parked in the shade.
    6. Each child was given a balloon by the clown.

C.
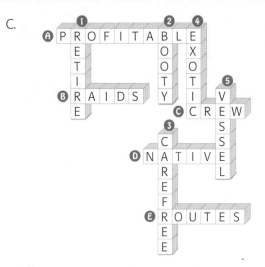

16 Pirates of the Caribbean (2)

A. 1. They became legendary ... North America.
    2. Piracy was taking ... countries.
    3. He was tall ... his chest.
    4. In one case ... evil he was.
    5. It was acts ... easy for him.
    6. A British naval ... North Carolina inlet.
    7. They then fought ... killed him.
    8. However, the governor ... pounds.
    9. With Blackbeard's death came the end of piracy.
    10. This paltry payment was hardly worth risking their lives.

B. 2. bleed ; will bleed
    3. began ; will begin
    4. come ; will come
    5. did ; will do
    6. think ; thought
    7. fought ; will fight
    8. lost ; will lose
    9. wear ; will wear
    10. wrote ; will write
    11. grow ; will grow
    12. shake ; shook

C. (Answers will vary.)

17 The Origins of the Written Words

A. 1 ; 2 ; 2 ; 1
B. 4 ; 5 ; 1 ; 2 ; 3
C. 1. is 2. She
    3. told 4. rang ; went
    5. were 6. play
    7. rings ; come 8. seated
    9. speak 10. offered

11. choose ; preferred 12. take
13. done 14. students ; having
D. (Answers will vary.)

Progress Test 2

A. 1. b 2. c 3. a 4. c
5. b 6. c 7. a 8. c
9. c 10. b 11. a 12. c
13. b
B. (Answers will vary.)
C. (Answers will vary.)
D. 1. "Is it cold outside?" she asked.
2. Sam's birthday was August 15, 1989.
3. "Stop, don't move!" screamed the police officer.
4. Dr. Smith worked for the Canadian Ministry of Health.
5. The small, frightened Siamese cat curled up in her lap.
6. On a recent trip to Montreal, his family went to watch the Expos.
7. Why do Canadians enjoy hockey so much, especially the Toronto Maple Leafs?
8. One day, he hoped to play basketball in the NBA, but first he would have to grow much taller.
E. 1. were ; finish 2. tell
3. were 4. viewed ; played
5. came ; lined ; take 6. was ; went
7. are ; require
F. 1. running 2. rises ; sets
3. satisfied 4. completed
5. guaranteed 6. replaceable
7. difference
8. swiftly ; defeated ; runner
9. sewed ; washed ; hung
10. swept ; covering
G. 1. flew 2. knew
3. went 4. thought
5. bought 6. built
7. did 8. tried
9. was 10. threw
H. 1.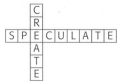

2.

3.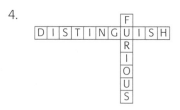

4.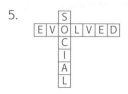

5.

6.

1 Nouns and Noun Use

A. 1. collective   2. proper   3. collective
   4. simple   5. compound   6. collective
   7. collective   8. simple   9. proper
   10. compound   11. simple   12. collective

B. 1. brother-in-law ; fireman
   2. classroom ; tomato plant ; window sill
   3. fire insurance
   4. bedroom ; fireplace
   5. seat belt
   6. flashlight
   7. baby-sitter
   8. grade eight ; high school
   9. motorcycle
   10. great-grandchild ; grandmother

C. 1. flock   2. army   3. navy
   4. group   5. audience   6. jury
   7. family   8. orchestra   9. crowd
   10. team   11. class   12. committee

D. 1. protects   2. visit   3. plays
   4. choose   5. applauds   6. find
   7. eat   8. go

E. 1. ships ; 1   2. knives ; 7   3. heroes ; 4
   4. countries ; 6   5. cowboys ; 5   6. bushes ; 2
   7. zoos ; 3

F. 1. singer   2. runner   3. dancer
   4. swimmer   5. hiker   6. teacher
   7. baker   8. climber   9. driver
   10. worker

Challenge
   1. artist   2. typist
   3. mathematician   4. author

2 Pronouns

A. 1. they   2. they   3. me
   4. their   5. it   6. they

B. 1. which   2. Which
   3. Where   4. this
   5. Those   6. When ; which
   7. Who; where / when   8. Where ; This

C. 1. which   2. which
   3. who   4. which
   5. who   6. which
   7. which   8. who

D. 1. ourselves   2. himself
   3. themselves   4. ourselves
   5. itself

Challenge
   1. myself –> me   2. myself –> I
   3. (Correct)   4. Delete "Myself"
   5. (Correct)   6. Himself –> He
   7. myself –> me
   No. 5

E. 1. Whose   2. my   3. I
   4. Whoever   5. me   6. us
   7. whom   8. I   9. whomever
   10. they ; we   11. yours

3 Descriptive Words and Phrases

A. 1. The <u>sly</u> fox slipped (quietly) through the woods.
   2. The <u>black</u> cloud hovered (menacingly) over the <u>playing</u> field.
   3. John, the <u>oldest</u> boy in the class, spoke (confidently).
   4. The boys (often) enjoyed playing <u>exciting</u> <u>computer</u> games.
   5. The <u>red</u> bicycle (suddenly) broke down in the middle of the trip.
   6. They (carefully) entered the <u>cold</u>, <u>dark</u> cave.

Challenge
   1. adjective   2. adverb
   3. adverb   4. adjective

B. 1. The walk <u>to the store</u> was very difficult (during the storm).
   2. (In the morning), the animals <u>in the barn</u> were fed.
   3. The leader <u>of the pack</u> was the large grey wolf.
   4. The pens <u>in the desk</u> were the property <u>of the boy</u> <u>in the third row</u>.
   5. (At the game), we ate our lunch <u>of sandwiches and cookies</u>.
   6. (During his speech), he dropped the notes <u>of the project</u>.

Challenge
   1. again   2. together   3. up
   4. back   5. up

C. 1. into   2. differed from   3. entered at
   4. stays at   5. among   6. with
   7. Besides   8. entered into   9. beside

D. (Suggested answers)
   1. annual   2. final   3. senior
   4. special   5. bright   6. sunny
   7. quickly   8. local   9. early
   10. challenging   11. silly   12. fun
   13. gladly   14. blue   15. hungry
   16. generously   17. huge   18. lucky
   19. clear   20. Suddenly   21. dark
   22. slowly   23. ferociously   24. wildly

4 Understanding Verb Forms

A. 1. makes   2. needed   3. wished
   4. play   5. arrived   6. is
   7. cost

B. 1. is   2. requires   3. is
   4. are   5. is   6. plays
   7. have   8. realize

C. 1. were   2. was   3. has
   4. is   5. has   6. are

D. 1. are ; are   2. was   3. wants
   4. want   5. agrees   6. has

E. 1. Active   2. Passive   3. Active
   4. Passive   5. Passive

F. 1. They <u>finished</u> their (homework) before going out to play.
   2. He <u>sailed</u> his (boat) across the lake.
   3. Whenever it is cold outside, she <u>wears</u> a heavy (sweater).
   4. If we don't play well, we <u>will lose</u> the (game).
   5. <u>Are</u> you <u>eating</u> your (dinner) now?
   6. He <u>ate</u> (meat) and (potatoes) for supper.

G. 1. watched – TR   2. was thrown – INT
    3. won – TR   4. watched – INT ; lost – TR
    5. arrived – INT ; unpacked – TR
    6. sang – INT ; were delighted – INT
    7. were – INT
Challenge
    1. Flowers were gathered from the garden by the children.
    2. Her friends were met by her at the bus stop.
    3. The scraps on the table were eaten by the dog.
    4. The clown entertained the children.

5 Verb Tenses

A. 1. Paula is walking to school instead of taking the bus.
    2. I have a new bicycle.
    3. She has been walking her dog in the park.
    4. We have been swimming in the lake.
    5. My friends and I are planning to have a party.
    6. My dog has been chasing the ball.
B. 1. were playing   2. shone
    3. had been arriving   4. had watched
    5. had been visiting   6. helped
    7. had done   8. were having
    9. had tried
C. 1. will wait   2. will have been played
    3. will have given   4. will go
    5. will have wanted   6. will watch out
    7. will have been congratulating
    8. will have paced
D. (Individual writing)
Challenge
    (Individual writing)

6 The Sentence and Its Parts

A. 2. The (cute) kitten | was playing (with a ball of wool).
    3. The (old) building | was being demolished (by the wrecking crew).
    4. The (uncertain) weather | caused a delay (in our plans).
    5. Water-skiing | is difficult if you are a beginner.
    6. We | walked two miles (to get to town).
    7. The (hot) sun | shines (brightly) (in the sky).
    8. I | was laughing (at the clown).
B. 1. An   2. the   3. the
    4. an   5. a   6. a
C. 1. lunch   2. (students) ; assignment
    3. (him) ; welcome   4. (children) ; treats
    5. (friend) ; truth 6. equipment
    7. (passengers) ; news   8. (us) ; ticket
    9. us
D. 1. morning ; school   2. water
    3. shore   4. class ; recess
    5. hill ; horizon ; ocean   6. night ; moonlight
E. 1. B   2. A   3. B
    4. A ; A   5. B ; B   6. B
Challenge
    1. A ; C ; B ; E ; G ; J
    2. A ; B ; D ; E ; G ; J

3. A ; C ; B ; D ; E ; J ; F ; J
4. A ; B ; E ; G ; J ; J ; J
5. A ; B ; D ; E ; A ; B ; D
6. C ; B ; D ; E ; F ; J ; I ; E
7. B ; E ; G ; J ; F

7 Compound and Complex Sentences

A. 1. and saw a squirrel climb a tree.
    2. so we could go out and play.
    3. because we all played games.
    4. if I study very hard for the test.
B. 1. IC   2. DC   3. DC   4. DC
    5. IC   6. IC   7. IC   8. DC
    9. IC   10. DC   11. DC   12. IC
    13. DC   14. IC
C. 1. clause   2. phrase   3. sentence
    4. clause   5. sentence   6. sentence
    7. phrase   8. clause
D. 1. ADV   2. ADV   3. ADJ
    4. ADV   5. ADJ   6. ADV
E. (Individual writing)
F. (Individual writing)

Progress Test 1

A. 1. simple   2. simple   3. simple
    4. compound   5. simple   6. collective
    7. proper   8. proper   9. compound
    10. collective   11. collective   12. collective
    13. proper   14. proper
B. 1. boats   2. oxen   3. women
    4. coaches   5. bushes   6. heroes
    7. wives   8. knives   9. zoos
    10. shoes   11. cliffs   12. ladies
C. 1. baker   2. creator   3. designer
    4. player   5. thinker   6. swimmer
    7. teacher   8. helper   9. planner
    10. builder   11. speaker   12. liar
D. 1. their   2. they   3. our
    4. its   5. them   6. their
    7. me
E. 1. Which – interrogative   2. Who – interrogative
    3. those – demonstrative   4. that – relative
    5. who – relative   6. herself – reflexive
F. 1. frightened ; loudly   2. tall ; completely
    3. cheerful ; happily   4. sly ; cleverly
    5. threatening ; menacingly
G. 1. The bird in the bush sang a song of the wild.
    2. (Under the carpet), he hid his gift of money.
    3. (In the middle of the night), it began raining.
    4. The choir of St. Michael's sang (in the church) (near the village).
H. 1. between   2. into   3. from
    4. in   5. on
I. 1. wishes   2. play   3. is
    4. want   5. makes   6. chooses
    7. write
J. 1. Patricia's father drove the car.
    2. I drew that picture on the wall.

3. The birthday cake was made by Sam's mother.
4. The tree in the backyard was planted by us.
5. The naughty children set off the alarm.
K. 1. transitive 2. intransitive 3. transitive
   4. intransitive 5. transitive 6. intransitive
L. 1. dog – D
   2. (her) – I ; address – D
   3. flowers – D
   4. (students) – I ; homework – D
   5. friend – D
   6. me – D
   7. (him) – I ; bike – D
M. 1. moonlight 2. table 3. rainfall
   4. movie 5. hill ; farmhouse
N. (Answers will vary.)
   1. The children stopped playing because they were too tired.
   2. I like mangoes but I don't like bananas.
   3. Jason is short but he can play basketball well.
   4. We can go there by subway or by bus.
   5. I will tell you if you don't tell anyone else.

8 Verbal, Participle, and Infinitive Phrases

A. 1. Jumping – Subj. 2. Falling – Subj.
   3. chewing – Obj. 4. Winning – Subj.
   5. sipping ; eating – Obj. 6. Singing ; dancing – Subj.
   7. making – Obj. 8. watching – Obj.
   9. Playing – Subj.
B. 1. To fly – noun 2. to speak – noun
   3. To write – noun 4. to play – adverb
   5. to come – adverb
C. 1. sleeping – giant 2. chewing – gum
   3. swaying – branches ; rustling – noises
   4. carrying – case 5. cutting – edge
D. 1. Waiting for a long time – lady
   2. climbing the stairs – man
   3. Thrilled with the outcome – winner
   4. playing in the gym – students
   5. Worried that he would be late for school – boy
   6. playing a classical tune – orchestra
   7. hoping not to get lost – He
   8. Delighted with the cake that she baked – girl
   9. Frightened by the bulldog – children
   10. carrying an umbrella – woman
   11. Hearing the bad news – actress
   12. chasing the birds – puppy
   13. Surrounded by police – robber
E. 2. Falling from a horse can be dangerous.
   3. Losing the first game upset the players.
   4. To laugh makes you feel much better when you are sad.
   5. He loves to sing in the shower.
   6. Exercising is good for both the mind and the body.
Challenge
(Individual writing)

9 Phrases – Noun, Gerund, Appositive, Absolute

A. 1. E ; Fine, colourful silk was used to make neckties.

2. F ; Hot, spicy sauce was spread on the pizza.
3. B ; She wore expensive, costume jewellery.
4. C ; Around the campfire, they told scary, ghost stories.
5. A ; Bright, colourful flags surrounded the Olympic Stadium.
6. D ; Warm, fuzzy blankets kept us warm all night long.
B. 1. Laughing out loud – A
   2. playing the piano in front of a crowd – B
   3. keeping the news a secret – D
   4. running around the track – B
   5. Sweeping the floors – A
   6. flying a kite – C
   7. Making muffins – A
C. (Individual writing)
D. 1. The cottage we rented, the one with the large front porch, has a nice beach.
   2. That dog, the one with the bushy tail, belongs to him.
   3. He wanted a bicycle, one with racing wheels, for his birthday.
   4. He chose the first seat, the one near the window, because it had a view.
   5. His sister, the one in grade three, is waiting for him at the front door of the school.
   6. He drove the other car, the green convertible, to work every day.
   7. The players, those who showed up on time, got the most playing time.
   8. Snowboarding, a sport for the young, has become very popular.
   9. Health, the thing we all desire, can be achieved by eating properly.
   10. Fatigue, the state of exhaustion, followed her completion of the marathon.
E. (Individual writing)
F. 1. The children are fully entertained, the clown having made funny balloons for everyone.
   2. He ran out of the house, his lunch being left behind.
   3. He roared down the ice, everyone trying to catch him.
   4. The ice cream melted, chocolate spilling everywhere.
   5. The teacher handed out the report cards, students waiting anxiously.
   6. They lined up for the penalty shot, soccer fans standing motionless.
   7. People running everywhere, the rainstorm unleashed a heavy downpour.
   8. Fans lining up for hours, the tickets for the rock concert finally went on sale.
G. 1. the dog sitting up begging
   2. the runners taking their marks
   3. The contestants holding their breath
   4. Skiers dotting the hillside
   5. The end of the game coming near

10 Run-On Sentences and Sentence Combining

A. (Answers will vary.)
   1. When lunch was ready, we ate in the kitchen.
   2. The door is wide open so someone must be home.
   3. Because he has cut his foot, he put a bandage on it.
   4. When the buzzer went, the game was over.

5. She read the book about a mystery that took place in England.
6. When the train arrived at the station, it was half an hour late.
7. The weather was fine so we had a game of baseball.
8. Since it was breezy, our kites flew high in the sky.

B. (Answers will vary.)
1. The hungry cat mewed because it wanted milk.
2. The shiny, new car was red.
3. He was a grade four student of St. Patrick's School.
4. She wore a yellow ski jacket.
5. You should raise your hand to answer questions.
6. There was plenty of mathematics homework.
7. The baseball game was delayed because of rain.
8. The children participated in the 100-metre race in the schoolyard.

C. (Answers will vary.)
1. The mouse was frightened because the cat was ready to pounce.
2. The snow was like powder so the skiing was excellent.
3. The bird built a nest with twigs and bits of straw.
4. He couldn't find his key so he was locked out of the house.
5. The little girl was crying because she thought that she was lost.
6. They sailed on an ocean liner and they had a wonderful vacation.
7. They went to the baseball game and ate peanuts and cracker jacks.
8. Because the dresser drawers were full, there was not enough room for his clothes.
9. The players drank water when there was a break in the game.
10. The morning dew melted when the sun came up.

D. (Answers may vary.)
   The Air Canada Centre is a large sports facility in downtown Toronto. Building of the centre started in 1997 and was finished in 1999. The Air Canada Centre is home to the Toronto Maple Leafs and the Toronto Raptors. The first hockey game played there was between the Toronto Maple Leafs and the Montreal Canadiens on February 20, 1999. The first Raptor game played in the Air Canada Centre was on February 21, 1999 against the Vancouver Grizzlies. Often there are special events, meetings, concerts, and community events going on there. The Air Canada Centre has 19,800 seats for basketball games and 18,800 seats for hockey games.

11 Punctuation (1)

A. 1. Look out! - exclamatory
2. What time is it? - interrogative
3. It was an unusually hot day. - declarative
4. What a hot day! - exclamatory
5. Never do that again. - imperative
6. Do as you are told. - imperative
7. Help! - exclamatory
8. It was nice of him to offer his help even though he was busy. - declarative
9. Do you know which team got the champion in yesterday's match? - interrogative

B. 1. couldn't   2. wouldn't   3. I would / I had
4. don't   5. can't   6. you will
7. doesn't   8. he would / he had
9. he's   10. shouldn't   11. let us
12. won't   13. isn't   14. I have
15. mustn't

C. 1. people's – 2   2. person's – 1
3. women's – 2   4. boys' – 3
5. players' – 3   6. boy's – 1
7. hers (no change)   8. class's – 4
9. Keats's – 4   10. geese's – 2
11. children's – 2   12. Dennis's – 4
13. babies' – 3   14. cat's – 1

Challenge
1. Paul's ; wasn't   2. It's ; o'clock ; isn't
3. can't ; '98   4. Susan's ; wasn't
5. she'll   6. Let's ; isn't
7. Paul's ; it's   8. I'd
9. Don't ; Louis's   10. What's

D.   The day arrived for our camping trip. We packed the following items: a tent, a flashlight, a sleeping bag, and a cooler. Our guide gave us this important advice: do not leave food around the tent after dark. He also explained: "It is important to respect nature and the animals of the woodlands. Remember, you are visiting their territory. Treat it as if it was your own." We left home at 6:30 a.m. and arrived at the campsite at 11:00. It took nearly two hours to set up camp because we had to take care of the following duties: clearing the site, hammering in the tent pegs, fetching water, and setting up a campfire.

12 Punctuation (2)

A. 1. She wanted to finish school, to go to college, and to get a good job. – 2
2. We worked, ate, slept, and awoke the next day before they arrived. – 2
3. We visited our relatives in Saskatoon, Alberta. – 4
4. His birthday was August 14, 1992. – 4
5. We ate soup, sandwiches, cake, and ice cream for lunch. – 1
6. Dad, will you drive me to my friend's house? – 3
7. Playing hockey, going skiing, and snowboarding are my favourite things to do. – 1
8. The Raptors, the Leafs, and the Argos all play in Toronto, Ontario. – 1 ; 4

B. 1. "What do you want to eat for supper?" his mother asked.
2. "I wish we had school during the summer," said Susan.
3. "Don't touch that wire!" screamed the electrician.
4. "Do you have any apples, pears, or oranges?" asked the lady.
5. "Be careful!" he shouted. "There are snakes, spiders, and rats in the pit."
6. "We have to go now," Danny said.

C. 1. While he was walking home,
2. while they cheered at the hockey game
3. After they watched the movie,
4. Whenever he runs in cold weather,
5. Because they were late,
6. If it rains tomorrow,

Challenge

"Is everyone ready?" asked Miss Jackson. She then announced, "The bus is waiting outside." The students put on their coats, picked up their knapsacks, pulled out their bus tickets, and formed a line. Whenever the students took a class trip, they were very excited. Today, they were going to visit the wax museum located in Niagara Falls, Ontario. The museum was very interesting because it had numerous famous people displayed in wax form. John Lennon, Elvis Presley, John F. Kennedy, and Pierre Elliot Trudeau were a few of the famous people on display. Because the wax figures were so lifelike, it was a very spooky experience. One of the students screamed, "That wax figure moved!" We all heard this and ran outside. Because we had now left the museum, the teacher suggested that we eat lunch. After lunch, we walked to the park, looked at the Falls, and returned to the bus. Although our trip was shortened by the scary incident, we had a good time.

D. 1. I bought her a birthday gift; it was something she needed.
2. Hockey is my favourite sport; I love to stick-handle the puck.
3. She was the smartest girl in the class; she always got the highest marks.
4. The teacher arrived late today; her car broke down.
5. Never before have we had such weather; the winds howled all night long.
6. It was a great celebration; we all ate cake and ice cream.
7. The students assembled in the gymnasium; the principal was going to speak to them.
8. The buses were running late; instead, we took the subway.
9. My dog loves to run; he really likes to fetch a ball.
10. Look up to the sky; you can see the Milky Way.
11. The dentist gave him a needle; his face went numb.

13 Capitalization, Abbreviation, and Quotation Marks

A. 1. Mr. and Mrs. Smith arrived in Toronto on the third of November.
2. He read "The Hobbit" by J.R.R. Tolkien.
3. "Harry Potter" books are very popular.
4. She visited her doctor, Dr. Johnson, whose office was on Main St.
5. At Christmas, the children sang "Jingle Bells".
6. We went to the SkyDome to see the Blue Jays play against the Minnesota Twins.
7. He watched a show entitled "Animals of Africa" on Discovery Channel.
8. On Monday, we have English class and on Wednesday, we have French class.
9. Elton John recorded "Goodbye England's Rose" as a tribute to Princess Diana.
10. We watched a Disney film entitled "Beauty and the Beast".
11. Mr. Todd Dixon, our teacher, brought his dog, Spot, to school.
12. Our computer runs on "Windows ME" with Microsoft Word.

B. 1. He worked for the Ministry of the Environment.

2. Doctor Richards had his office in the CN Tower.
3. We boarded a plane for our trip to eastern Europe.
4. He lived in the east end of Toronto.
5. My aunt Hilda's moved out West; I will visit her next fall.
6. Uncle Adam worked for Parks and Recreation for the town of Ajax.
7. My teacher was known as Professor Sanderson when he taught at Oxford University.
8. When we were in eastern Europe, we travelled to Italy and enjoyed Italian food.
9. My uncle, Professor Jones, sent a letter to the Premier of Ontario, Mike Harris.
10. The Chunnel connects Britain and France.
11. Which planet is bigger, Venus or Mars?
12. I went to Metro Zoo with Uncle Tommy yesterday.

C. 1. cm.   2. oz.   3. mm.   4. qt.
5. lb.   6. ft.   7. in.   8. mi.
9. km.   10. kg.   11. L.   12. ml.
13. Sun.   14. Mon.   15. Tues.   16. Wed.
17. Thurs.   18. Fri.   19. Sat.   20. Jan.
21. Feb.   22. Mar.   23. Apr.   24. May
25. Jun.   26. Jul.   27. Aug.   28. Sept.
29. Oct.   30. Nov.   31. Dec.   32. yr.

D. 1. She said, "Please help me lift the boxes."
2. "What time is it?" he asked.
3. I read the short story "A Monkey's Paw" by W.W. Jacobs.
4. We found travel information in the magazine article "Skiing in the Rockies".
5. The teacher stated, "Homework is due for tomorrow."
6. The movie "The Wizard of Oz" is a family favourite.
7. "Where are you going for your summer holidays?" asked our teacher.
8. We were singing along to "Happy Birthday to You" at the party.
9. "Don't you know the answer?" asked Teddy.
10. "Last Christmas" by George Michael is a nice song.
11. Can you tell me who wrote "Julius Caesar"?

14 Tips for Effective Writing

A. 1. He will wait until the train arrives.
2. They travelled across Canada by car.
3. Before the game, no fans had arrived.
4. I think she should be chosen as the class representative.
5. Now we will leave for school.
6. Because it was his birthday, there was a big party.
7. He would often walk to school alone.
8. Although he won the race, he was still not happy.

B. 1. past → passed   2. hole → whole
3. there → their ; pair → pear
4. principle → principal   5. presence → presents
6. weak → week   7. Who's → Whose
8. whether → weather   9. Its → It's
10. they're → their

C. (Answers will vary.)
1. John has expensive, new skates.
2. George has a part-time job working at the variety store.

3. When the rain stopped and the sun came out, we continued to play the game.
4. He won the award for top student given at the assembly.
5. Barbados is a coral island in the Caribbean.
6. Toronto is a large city with a population of nearly three million.
7. The large, brick house had a swimming pool.
8. Kara attends a high school that has 1,100 students.
9. The tall, thin boy is rushing out of the dark, stuffy room.

D. (Answers will vary.)
1. The teacher didn't have any chalk left.
2. Ian told Gerry that it wasn't any of his business.
3. Amanda can't tell anybody about what happened.
4. "Don't give me any more work to do," he exclaimed.
5. She didn't have any idea what time it was.
6. I can't find anything in the drawer.
7. The children weren't going anywhere after school.
8. "Don't do anything for the time being," he said.

15 The Descriptive Paragraph

A. (Individual writing)
B. (Individual writing)
C. (Individual writing)
D. (Individual writing)

Progress Test 2

A. 1. noun   2. noun   3. adjective
   4. adjective   5. noun   6. adjective
B. 1. filled with flowers   2. waiting for the bus
   3. Laughing at the clown   4. running across the road
   5. waving fans   6. burning house
C. (Individual writing)
D. (Suggestions only)
1. Don't ask questions; you should listen to all the information first.
2. We woke up early, packed our bags, jumped in the car and left.
3. The students went to the zoo; they saw exotic animals. It was a great day.
4. The circus came to town. They had many great acts and we enjoyed them.
5. At recess, boys play basketball and girls play volleyball.
E. (Suggestions only)
1. The hungry students ate lunch in the park.
2. The dog barked at the friendly mailman.
3. The cold night came and the wind blew.
4. Susan, a student new to our school, came today.
5. Hockey is a popular sport in Canada.
F. 1. ? ; interrogative   2. ! ; exclamatory
   3. . ; declarative   4. ? ; interrogative
   5. . ; imperative   6. ! ; exclamatory
   7. ? ; interrogative
G. 1. won't   2. didn't   3. hasn't   4. we're
   5. she's   6. we've   7. can't   8. couldn't
   9. wasn't   10. they're   11. I'm   12. he's
   13. it's   14. don't

H. 1. :   2. ;   3. ;   4. :
   5. : ;   6. : ;   7. :   8. ;
I. 1. people's   2. hers   3. Louis's
   4. doctors'   5. player's   6. players'
   7. class's   8. men's
J. 1. On July 10, 2003, they will celebrate an anniversary and go out for dinner.
2. Although they were the first to arrive, no one noticed them.
3. Jeff asked, "Is the appointment for August 2, 2002, or is it for a later date?"
4. The tool kit included: a wrench, a hammer, nails, and a screwdriver.
5. Unless you change the time, no one will be able to attend the meeting.
6. Hammerhead, Peter's bulldog, is very playful in spite of his fierce look.
K. 1. Sam asked, "Who will be on my team?"
2. We went to see "Beauty and the Beast".
3. We sang "Happy Birthday to You".
4. Sasha stated, "I don't think I can go swimming today."
5. Our class read the short story "A Day on the Farm".
6. "We could have won the game," said the dejected captain.
L. 1. He's the best player on our team but he doesn't know it.
2. He borrowed Paul's book and hasn't returned it yet.
3. It's about time you took your dog to get its new collar.
4. When it's time to go, you'll know it.
5. He wasn't always a student at our school; he arrived in '99.
M. The Grade six students were looking eagerly forward to Friday. Ms Patterson, their teacher, promised to take them to the Science Centre. However, the children had to do some research first. "You should work in groups of three or four, and each group has to find the information on this worksheet," explained Ms Patterson. "Can we get it from the Internet?" asked Jenny. "Sure," answered Ms Patterson, "but you must double check the information because not all the information on the Net is accurate."

1 The Topic Sentence

A. 1. C   2. B
   3. A   4. A
B. (Answers will vary.)
C. (Answers will vary.)
D. (Answers will vary.)

2 Following the Topic Sentence

A. (Answers will vary.)
B. (Answers will vary.)
C. (Answers will vary.)

3 Descriptive Language (1)

A. 1. lodge   2. mansion
   3. ferocious   4. (an) interesting
   5. comedian   6. lanky
   7. convertible   8. lighthouse
   9. sprinter   10. gourmet
B. 1. sauntered   2. rushed
   3. leaped   4. swooped
   5. zigzagged   6. slammed
   7. drifted   8. flashed
   9. blazed   10. devoured
C. 1. instantaneous   2. gingerly
   3. roared   4. voyage
   5. precarious   6. refreshing
   7. sleek   8. executed
   9. complications   10. undulating
   11. efficiently   12. floated
   13. gracefully   14. careening
   15. shrieked / roared
D. (Sentences will vary.)
   1. singing   2. dining
   3. running   4. crying
   5. speaking   6. fishing
   7. swimming   8. driving
   9. burning   10. falling

4 Confusing Words

A. 1. noticeable   2. definite
   3. success   4. heroes
   5. occurrence   6. necessary
   7. receive   8. therefore
   9. professor   10. argument

B. 1. their   2. presents
   3. hole   4. passed
   5. Who's   6. sight
   7. weak   8. duel
   9. fourth   10. loose
   11. alter   12. bear
   13. bear   14. herd
   15. patients   16. principal
   17. plane ; plain   18. council ; counsel
   19. hoarse   20. diary
   21. fare ; fair   22. break
   23. peace   24. course
   25. bored
C. 1. this   2. these
   3. This   4. Those
   5. this   6. these
   7. Those   8. them
   9. That
D. 1. good   2. bad
   3. good   4. bad
   5. badly   6. good
E. 1. fewer   2. less
   3. Fewer   4. fewer
   5. less   6. fewer

5 Creating a Story Ending

A. (Answers will vary.)
B. 1. mid-June
   2. located at the track and field meet
C. Major : Lisa, Jennifer
   Minor : the announcer, the starter, other competitors, the crowd
D. (Answers will vary.)
   1. The scorching sun blazed down on the competitors.
   2. They arched their backs and lowered their heads.
   3. The crowd cheered wildly.
   4. She stumbled and sprawled.
E. (Answer will vary.)
   This is a story about two highly competitive runners that compete against each other at a championship track meet. While running neck and neck, one of the runners stumbles.
F. (Answer will vary.)
   There is conflict between the two runners, Lisa and Jennifer. There is also conflict between Lisa and herself as she must have the courage to recover from her accident.

G. (Answer will vary.)

 The suspense is first built up with the two runners preparing to race. Further suspense is built when the runners are neck and neck after 30 metres into the race. Suspense continues when Lisa stumbles.

H. (Answer will vary.)

6 Word-Building Challenge

A. (Answers will vary.)
 1. engagement ; disengage
  Best synonym : occupy
 2. occurrence ; occurred
  Best synonym : happen
 3. enrage ; raging
  Best synonym : fury
 4. production ; producer
  Best synonym : make
 5. neglectful ; negligence
  Best synonym : ignore
 6. identified ; identical
  Best synonym : self

B. 1. fad
 3. omit
 5. yield
 2. individuality
 4. transpire
 6. monopolize

C. 1. bearable
 3. incapable
 5. well-known
 7. difficult
 9. incredible
 2. important
 4. disgusting
 6. stubborn
 8. dangerous
 10. pitiful

D. 1 a. stare b. stair
 2 a. core b. corps
 3 a. pores b. pours
 4 a. break b. brake
 5 a. red b. read
 6 a. night b. knight
 7 a. allowed b. aloud
 8 a. rain b. reign
 9 a. way b. weigh
 10 a. sail b. sale

7 Descriptive Language (2)

A. 1. hazardous
 3. spacious
 5. challenging
 7. deafening
 9. dove
 2. glad
 4. hideous
 6. pace
 8. glided

B. 1. K
 3. M
 5. O
 7. A
 9. P
 11. E
 13. H
 15. J
 2. L
 4. N
 6. C
 8. F
 10. D
 12. G
 14. I
 16. B

C. (Suggestions only)
 1. abundance
 3. bleak
 5. ornate
 7. obscure
 9. cantankerous
 11. intrigued
 13. coincidental
 15. logical
 2. jeering
 4. energetic
 6. obstinate
 8. consecutive
 10. grievance
 12. absurd
 14. grimace

Progress Test 1

A. 1. C
 3. B
 5. C
 2. A
 4. B

B. 1. H
 3. G
 5. C
 7. A
 9. F
 2. I
 4. B
 6. D
 8. J
 10. E

C. 1. F
 3. I
 5. C
 7. D
 9. J
 2. G
 4. B
 6. H
 8. E
 10. A

D. 1. E
 3. A
 5. C
 7. D
 9. C
 11. E
 13. D
 15. B
 2. D
 4. B
 6. B
 8. E
 10. A
 12. C
 14. A

E. 1. I ; noticeable
 3. I ; therefore
 5. I ; receive
 7. C
 9. I ; professor
 2. C
 4. I ; necessary
 6. I ; heroes
 8. C
 10. I ; occurrence

F. 1. their
 3. Whose
 2. presence
 4. plane

5. herd
7. bored
6. principal
8. fair
G. 1. this
3. well
5. bad
7. less
9. fewer
2. Those
4. good
6. badly
8. less
10. less
H. 1. decide
3. rage
5. neglect
2. occur
4. produce
6. identity
I. 1. C
3. A
5. D
7. J
9. G
2. E
4. I
6. B
8. F
10. H
J. 1. dangerous
3. hideous
5. deafening
2. spacious
4. challenging
6. floated
K. 1. pours
3. red / reed
5. allowed
7. way
2. brake
4. knight
6. reign
8. sale
L. (Answers will vary.)

8 The Columbia Icefield

A. 1. gradual
3. harsh
5. environment
7. approximately
9. boundary
11. establish
13. venture
15. enforced
17. conservation
2. traction
4. breath-taking
6. accessible
8. situated
10. accumulated
12. base
14. detectable
16. designed

B. (Answers will vary.)
Paragraph One :
1. The Columbia Icefield is located on the boundary of Jasper and Banff national parks.
2. The Icefield is 350 metres thick.
Paragraph Two :
1. Tourists take a Snocoach out onto the glacier.
2. The Icefield is made up of falling snow that has accumulated for over 400 years.
Paragraph Three :
1. Grizzly bears have winter dens near the Icefield.
2. Strict rules of conservation are enforced to protect plants and animals.

Paragraph Four :
1. Thousands of people visit the Icefield each year.
2. This region has wildlife, rivers, mountains, and lakes for tourists to enjoy.
C. (Answers will vary.)

9 Haiku Poetry

A. (Answers will vary.)
B. (Answers will vary.)
C. (Answers will vary.)
D. (Answer will vary.)

10 Narrative Writing

A. (Answers will vary.)
B. (Answers will vary.)

11 Vocabulary Development

A. 1. stampede
3. trial
5. cyclist
7. collision
9. captive
11. fixture
13. coincident
15. snowmobile
17. natural
19. automatic
2. relative
4. campsite
6. attraction
8. nonsense
10. victorious
12. repair
14. collection
16. coincidental
18. comical
20. rearrange

B. (Answers will vary.)
1. Mary called her friend on the telephone but she got no answer.
2. As soon as the game was over, everyone went home.
3. If you come over to my house, we can play computer games.
4. The sun came out after the storm was over.
5. He waited for hours for his friends to show up but it started to get dark.
6. When the school bell rang, summer holidays had started.
7. Because he was the team captain, he had to be a leader.
8. After they ate dinner, they had dessert.
9. His new bike was very fast but it was too big for him.

10. Although his alarm went off, he was late for school.
11. Even though they were the first to arrive, they still waited a long time in line.
12. They were camping in the mountains when a bear visited their campsite.

C. (Answers will vary.)
D. (Answers will vary.)

12 Expository Writing

A. (Answers will vary.)
1. To instruct the reader as to the best way to establish a campfire
2. Although sitting around a campfire is one of the great joys of camping, building a long lasting, roaring campfire is not a simple task.
3. At this point you should be enjoying a roaring fire but be mindful to add wood consistently to maintain enough fuel to keep your fire going.

B. (Answers will vary.)
1. To explain to the reader that there are many interesting and fun things to do in the city during the summer
2. However, the city offers a variety of interesting ways to spend the hot, lazy days of summer.
3. Whatever your preference, the city in the summer is a lively place with something for everyone.

Challenge
(Answer will vary.)
C. (Answer will vary.)
D. (Answer will vary.)

13 Le Tour de France

Paragraph One :
1. B   2. A
3. C
(Individual writing of the sentence)
Paragraph Two :
1. B   2. E
3. C   4. D
5. A
(Individual writing of the sentence)
Paragraph Three :
1. D   2. E
3. C   4. A
5. G   6. F
7. H   8. B
(Individual writing of the sentence)

Paragraph Four :
1. C   2. H
3. D   4. A
5. F   6. G
7. E   8. B
(Individual writing of the sentence)
Paragraph Five :
1. E   2. C
3. D   4. B
5. A
(Individual writing of the sentence)

14 Informal Writing

A. (Answer will vary.)
B. (Answer will vary.)
C. (Answer will vary.)
D. (Answers will vary.)

15 Synonyms – Facts about Canada

hoisted – 2 ; establishing – 1 ; sovereignty – 3 ; ceded – 4 ; official – 5

originated – 7 ; officially – 10 ; acknowledged – 8 ; maritime – 6 ; original – 13 ; declared – 9 ; version – 11 ; designed – 14 ; symbol – 12

territory – 18 ; extends – 15 ; expanse – 19 ; astounding – 17 ; remarkably – 16 ; diverse – 20

impressive – 25 ; inception – 24 ; accessible – 26 ; transported – 27 ; employed – 21 ; sector – 22 ; opportunities – 28 ; emerge – 23 ; particularly – 29

density – 31 ; unique – 32 ; Primary – 30 ; unprecedented – 33 ; optimistic – 34

initial – 37 ; prior – 39 ; composer – 41 ; accompany – 42 ; numerous – 38 ; renditions – 40 ; unaltered – 35 ; minor – 36

Progress Test 2

A. 1. located   2. area
   3. bottom   4. nearly
   5. approachable   6. wander
   7. grip   8. earned
   9. slow   10. visible
  11. set up   12. rough

13. surroundings   14. protection
15. applied   16. created
B. (Answers will vary.)
C. 1. state   2. coincide
  3. relate   4. attract
  5. capture   6. collide
  7. sense   8. incidence
  9. victory   10. repair
D. (Answers will vary.)
  1. He walked home because he missed the school bus.
  2. She invited her friends over for a sleepover and they ordered pizza.
  3. The game continued although it was raining.
  4. She set the table while he cooked hot dogs.
  5. As soon as the students were seated at their desks, the teacher began teaching.
E. Group A :
  1. I   2. J
  3. E   4. C
  5. G   6. A
  7. H   8. D
  9. F   10. B
  Group B :
  1. G   2. E
  3. A   4. I
  5. B   6. J
  7. C   8. F
  9. H   10. D
F. 1. C   2. E
  3. B   4. D
  5. I   6. H
  7. F   8. G
  9. A   10. J
G. (Answers will vary.)
H. (Answer will vary.)

1.

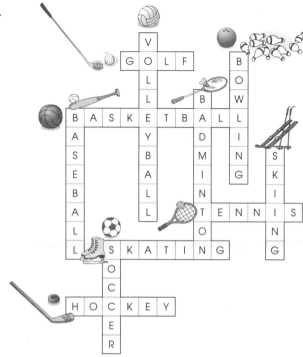

2. (Suggested slides)

main → rain → gain → grin → grip → trip → trap

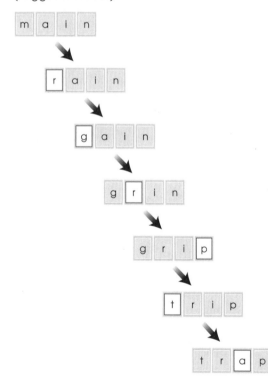

3.

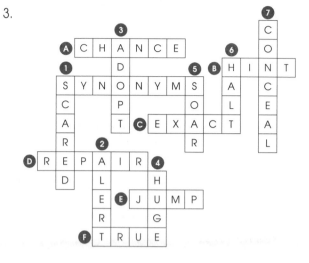

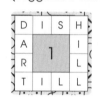

A C H A N C E

B H I N T

C O N C E A L

S Y N O N Y M S

C E X A C T

D R E P A I R

E J U M P

F T R U E

4. (Suggested answers)

D I S H		K I N G	
DART · 1 · ILL		KICK · 2 · ATE	
TILL		KITE	

P E E L		H A I R	
PORT · 3 · LIVE		HOPE · 4 · EARS	
TAKE		EVER	

T H A T		L I L Y	
TAIL · 5 · AIC		LAKE · 6 · YARN	
LOOK		EARN	

5. WE LIVE ON A PLANET FAR AWAY FROM EARTH. WE WANT TO MAKE NEW FRIENDS. CAN WE BE FRIENDS?

6.

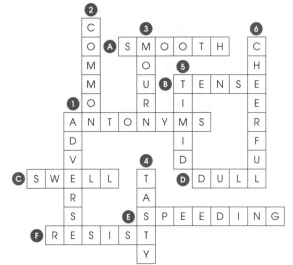

7. (Suggested slides)

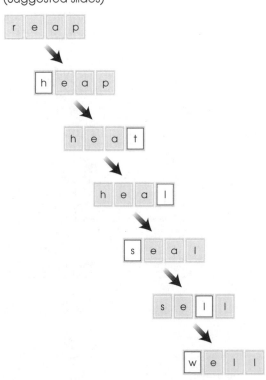

8.

h	c	d	l	f	j	a	n	e	m	g	a	e
f	r	m	g	w	w	h	q	b	a	n	h	b
c	i	c	a	d	a	c	n	s	n	e	j	l
d	c	h	m	o	s	q	u	i	t	o	c	a
m	k	b	o	b	p	e	p	d	i	g	o	d
k	e	p	f	l	b	i	l	g	s	l	c	y
r	t	l	d	j	e	n	f	a	j	c	k	b
c	a	o	v	c	e	u	r	o	t	p	r	u
h	f	c	l	p	t	z	x	i	v	b	o	g
d	b	u	m	b	l	e	b	e	e	i	a	c
a	k	s	e	f	e	i	y	a	m	q	c	i
j	m	t	d	o	q	l	r	m	o	t	h	m
k	a	n	a	n	t	x	b	c	s	r	o	g

9.

10. 1. honeycomb   2. houseboat
    3. starfish   4. bookworm
    5. firecracker   6. keystone

11.

g	i	r	p	d	o	j	g	t	d	q	s	f	j
k	u	a	x	k	c	l	r	p	e	n	c	i	l
e	r	q	f	n	h	n	i	x	q	b	i	s	k
p	u	l	m	o	s	d	y	q	c	o	s	n	t
c	l	i	p	t	w	m	b	v	z	h	s	a	i
n	e	g	y	e	r	a	s	e	r	q	o	p	r
s	r	o	p	b	a	l	b	p	u	j	r	x	c
d	h	t	j	o	n	x	c	u	z	e	s	m	w
c	r	a	y	o	n	z	t	n	d	y	f	v	t
e	p	y	m	k	i	g	o	c	v	z	r	h	u
k	b	v	s	z	l	v	k	h	b	g	o	n	e
p	i	u	w	h	k	s	t	a	p	l	e	r	m
e	c	m	j	x	w	o	u	l	w	u	j	a	f
n	r	f	y	a	e	s	p	a	p	e	r	q	b

12.

Across:
- **(A)** LOSS
- **(B)** RIGID
- **(C)** HARMFUL
- **(D)** PLANT
- **(E)** COLD
- **(F)** FRAGILE
- **(G)** EXTENSIVE
- **(top)** SYNONYMS

Down:
- **(1)** PECULIAR
- **(2)** SWF...
- **(3)** ... SOCIABLE
- **(4)** CI...
- **(5)** ...
- **(6)** ... LUCKY
- **(7)** ...

Grid:
```
P   S Y N O N Y M S
E   W         L O S S
C B R I G I D   C   I   O
U   F       C H A R M F U L
D P L A N T     P       I
  I         S   A   E C O L D
  A         O   B       U
  R         C   L       C
    F R A G I L E       K Y
            A
            B
            L
        G E X T E N S I V E
```

15.

Across:
- **(A)** TOUGH
- **(B)** MURMUR
- **(C)** DEPART
- **(D)** INNOCENT
- **(E)** INCREASE
- **(F)** STRESSFUL
- **(top)** ANTONYMS

Down:
- COMBINE
- OCCUPIED
- HAZARD...
- OPTIMISTIC

Grid:
```
A T O U G H             O
        U     A Z   5   P
1       A N T O N Y M S T
C   2   I     H         I
O   C   Q     A         M
B M U R M U R R         I
B I   E   C D E P A R T S
I T       E       E     T
N I N N O C E N T       I
E C       I       S     C
    I E I N C R E A S E
    Z
F S T R E S S F U L
```

13. (Suggested slides)

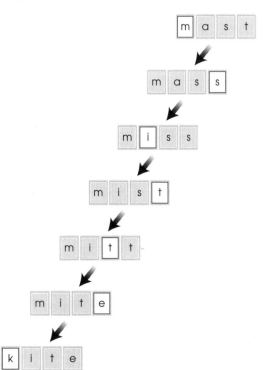

mast → mass → miss → mist → mitt → mite → kite

14. I dreamt that I skied with Santa Claus last night.

16.

Word search grid:
```
l n p h d i b g r q y [p] e n
x f H m a e z s w o l  u  h o
[c] t a n m c H a m h z [m] j c
o b k j y p l n x w i  p  u g
s h d (g) m o j [t r i c k] g t
t k a w h e q r e l q  i  H a
u [H a l l o w e e n] t  n  m k
m d f z t p s a y i p  q  w f
e o h t l c n t w s b  a  e j
[s p i d e r] h s g i a  c  x o
b f n y q [s k e l e t o n] m
p j f x l b z k x d s c  p  r
d z w a r c i g b r f z  h  l
m l x i q j n p o m k y  m  k
```

Words found: pen, pumpkin, cat, trick, Halloween, spider, skeleton, ghost, bat